I0034050

An Accounts Payable Back-to-Work Action Plan

Tactics Every Organization Should Use when Returning from the COVID-19 Crisis (or Any Other Crisis)

Mary S. Schaeffer, AP Now

Note: Parts of this book have previously been published in the Accounts Payable Now & Tomorrow monthly newsletter, some of Mary S. Schaeffer's other books, and in AP Now surveys and special reports.

Copyright © 2020 Mary S. Schaeffer
All rights reserved.

ISBN: 978-1-7351000-0-5

CONTENTS

ACKNOWLEDGMENTS

This book would not have come to pass were it not for the horrific COVID-19 crisis and with the insights shared at our weekly AP Isolation sessions by the professionals who work in or are responsible for the accounts payable function. A big round of applause for those who came to those weekly sessions and shared their insights, comments and questions. Not only did you enlighten everyone, often you gave us a much-needed laugh.

I'd also like to take this opportunity to acknowledge a huge debt of gratitude to the AP Association, a global organization headquartered in the UK, and its CEO, Jamie Radford, for collaborating with my organization, AP Now, on those weekly AP Isolation events. You made them better for your insights and a lot of fun to give in a time when joy was in short supply.

I would be remiss if I did not mention Lynn Larson, who was a huge help in getting this project completed in record time—even my desire for speed did not match precisely with her penchant for attention to detail. And last, but definitely not least, my husband Hal, who as I write this is out in a mask and rubber gloves trying to procure dinner for us. What a strange, albeit exciting, world we live in.

PREFACE

Coronavirus, shelter-in-place, COVID-19, quarantine, isolation, lockdown, and pandemic were not part of our everyday vocabulary at the end of 2019. Even if we knew what some of those terms meant, we never thought of them in connection with the accounts payable function. All that changed in late winter 2020.

In late 2018, AP Now conducted a survey on Remote Workers in Accounts Payable. I had run a seminar in October of that year and a few of the attendees reported they had started having staffers were from home one or more days a week, if they wished. Not only did employee morale improve, but so did productivity. This was the genesis of the survey. Our timing was auspicious but it gave us something to compare behavior to during the crisis.

At the time we conducted that first survey, well over half did not allow staff to work from home except in cases of emergency. Must to my surprise, almost one-quarter, did allow employees to work from home, if they wished. These folks had a huge advantage when the shelter-in-place orders came down as they had the technology in place and knew how to make it work. Fast forward to the end of March when the AP Now studies show almost 85% of all accounts payable staffers were working from home. Some, in organizations that were heavily based in paper, were deemed to be essential workers and as such, were going into the office.

During the crisis, AP Now resolved to run one free webinar each week, as our tiny contribution to helping keep the morale of the accounts payable community up. We were joined in that effort by the AP Association, a global organization headquartered in the UK. Each of the sessions were run by Jamie Radford, CEO of the AP Association and myself.

In addition to the educational content we tried to share, we also tried to inject a little bit of fun. One of the ways we did this was to poll the audience on various issues. You will see the results of some of those polls throughout this book. Attendees at these sessions were quite generous in sharing their experiences and problems they encountered as we all plodded through this new working environment.

The foundation for the book is the 25-step action plan presented in the first chapter. Clearly not every organization will have every issue discussed, but you will have many. There's no way, for example, to avoid the ugliness of the frauds that popped up during the crisis. Criminals of all stripe look to take advantage of uncertainty. Virtually no organization had its accounts payable staff working completely remotely before the crisis. So, everyone will have the pains associated with developing a fair and equitable policy.

The following chapters break down the business intelligence around each of the issues raised in the initial plan. They present best practices adapted for the COVID-19 crisis and the work place that is likely to emerge afterwards. It operates from the position that a crisis of this sort is likely to happen again. What it will be and when it will happen are the big unknown. But one thing is certain. We need to do a better job in preparing. There is no excuse for not being prepared.

This starts with the new workplace. It looks at adapting a remote working policy, starting with steps every organization should do. It also discusses some changes that are likely to happen and reminds readers that in all likelihood, there will be greater diversity in the way organizations structure their accounts payable function.

The book then moves on to discuss the fundamental function of the accounts payable team: invoice processing. It looks at ways invoice processing needs to change, how organizations can move away from paper invoices requiring, at a minimum requiring that invoices be emailed, how they can start an invoice automation program and how they can increase usage of an existing one.

From that point, the book starts looking at the issues of duplicates. Before the crisis, there was a problem of vendors emailing duplicate copies of an invoice. Now, complicated by the issues surrounding remote working, the nightmare has gotten worse. A discussion on practices to address this headache is included. The book then moves on to address some questionable practices being used by vendors that could result in a duplicate payment. Suggestions on how to address the duplicate payment matter follow.

Of course, one of the biggest headaches for accounts payable teams during the crisis, is how to get paper checks issued. It highlighted the advantages of having an electronic payment program. Of course, this is one issue that is predominantly a US issue, as other countries don't rely on paper checks nearly as much as the US. The book has two chapters on starting and expanding an ACH program. It also takes a look at ACH debits, which while not used as frequently as ACH credits, were used as a last resort by some companies. The book has some suggestions for those who took this approach.

Electronic payments aren't the only alternative to paper checks. Cards can also be used and so there are some insights included on expanding a card program. The book then moves on to address two issues related to cards. The first is the matter of the special card issues created or intensified by the COVID-19 crisis and the second is the new expense reporting issues likely to be created during the mess.

Related to expense reporting is the huge issue of refunds. While this might have been a minor issue prior to the crisis, it has turned into a huge headache for those responsible. The book identifies all the potential issues and shares some suggestions for dealing with them.

Before turning to a look at fraud, there are some overall suggestions on going paperless. Then we take a look at fraud and some of the problems any organization might encounter. This is followed by a discussion of passwords and recommendations on what to do when you return to work.

Before closing, 1099s, payment audits and financing are addressed. The book concludes with a chapter on changes we are all likely to see and a look at lessons learned. As you read through the topics listed and some of the commentary, you might note that in addition to being a guide map to getting your accounts payable function working in tip top shape after the crisis, this is also a guide for some accounts payable process improvements.

We'll end this with a closing thought from Winston Churchill, "Never let a good crisis go to waste!"

CHAPTER 1: THE ACTION PLAN

The current crisis has been a wakeup call for many organizations, and more specifically, their accounts payable function. Many moved their AP function from their offices to their employees' homes with literally two days' notice. For most, the move was not smooth or pretty. Others found themselves mired in processes that were so paper driven, their accounts payable staffers were labeled critical and had to come into the office to work.

On March 19, just as the full extent of the crisis was beginning to become understood and companies were starting to seriously shelter at home, AP Now polled a group of its readers. It found that a full 84% of them were already isolating or were planning to start within the next few days. The main reason people weren't was that their organizations were so paper-dependent they were designated as essential. Figure 1 below shows the breakdown of the responses.

Quarantine Life Stats: 84% Working or Will Start Working from Home

Source: AP Now webinar attendees

AP Now

Figure 1. Working from Home

If your accounts payable staff was not able to work remotely, then consider the steps below which will help position your accounts payable team to be able to work remotely should this happen again.

Lessons Learned

We've learned several things through this process. For starters, the accounts payable function is critical for any organization from a business continuity standpoint. More care needs to be given to it. Additionally, most were woefully unprepared for that happening.

It is critical that when we go back, organizations review the work that done to ensure fraud and duplicate payments did not occur and also that everyone who should have been paid was paid. And pretty quickly, it will be necessary to create processes that will enable the accounts payable function to function the next time something like this happens, for it will. It is not a matter of if it will happen, but rather, when.

Let's take a look at the steps every organization should take when workers return to your physical location.

Steps Related to Reopening

Step 1: Expect the first day to be less productive as people get reacquainted with their co-workers. Think of it as you would when a popular staffer returns from a long vacation or hospital stay. 35% of attendees at one AP Isolation event said that the thing they missed most about their old work life was chatting with their co-workers.

So, even though you may be chomping at the bit to get started with your long list of tasks and changes you want to make, wait. Give the staff the time they need to get reacquainted and catch up after this ordeal Consider bringing donuts for coffee time or perhaps ordering a pizza for lunch.

Step 2: If any of your employees have issues that you even suspect might have HR implications, get someone from HR involved immediately. Do not make these decisions yourself. We're bound to run into issues that we did not address in the past. For example, if your state reopens businesses early and one or more of your employees believes their health is at risk, should you let them continue working from home? I think so, but you might be setting a precedent that is not inline with company policy.

So, consult HR at even the slightest provocation. I suspect there will be issues we have not thought of yet, so be prepared for the unexpected.

Steps Related to Invoices

Step 3: Adopt a policy of encouraging 100% submission of invoices either by email or through an invoice automation portal. Paper invoices, unless there is a legal requirement to have an original physical hard copy, should be discouraged at all costs. We expect in the near future those requirements will be changed,

According to a recent AP Now survey, about 27% of all invoices are received through the mail. This is too big a chunk to simply ignore during isolation. Therefore, it is imperative that companies take a hard stance on getting electronic copies of their invoices, wherever possible. Should vendor balk at this requirement remind them that next time there is a quarantine requirement, you might not be able to get them paid if they insist on sending paper.

Step 4: If using invoice automation, and usage is tepid, you need to take action. This is no longer acceptable. One of the many benefits of invoice automation is that the invoice is received electronically. As everyone learned the hard way, postal delivery of invoices creates a huge problem if the staff is forced to work remotely.

Investigate why the solution is not being used and take a hardline approach when you figure out the underlying cause. If employees do not know how to use it or are not comfortable using it, get them additional training. If employees are discouraging vendors from using it, have a little chat with the employee in question. If vendors are refusing to use it, find out why and address it. This last one may require the involvement of procurement.

Step 5: Once you have everything up and running and are beginning to plan for a possible future crisis, evaluate whether an invoice automation solution might be right for your organization. These solutions will not necessarily replace your processing staff, but rather act as a complimentary tool. Plus, the price of many of the models have come down and many are quite user-friendly.

Step 6: Double check for duplicate invoices sent during the crisis. Some vendors automatically send more than one and we fear a few amped up this practice when cash flow dried up. Whether the cause is an honest mistake or an outright deception, it does not matter. Your organization is under no obligation to pay an invoice twice. And if you do, immediately request that the vendor return the funds.

Create a process, if you don't already have one, of calling vendors who send multiple copies and request they send only one copy. They will probably agree to do so on the phone, but this is not a guarantee they will. Also, they may stop for a while and then resume the practice. (grrr) Finally, just when you think you have this issue semi-under-control, different vendors will start sending multiple copies of invoices. Do not expect this problem to go away any time soon, but do expect it to get worse in the short run.

Steps Related to Payments

Step 7: Review your processes for uncovering duplicate payments. Don't skip the review when you return because you have so much on your plate. The odds are quite high that many accounts payable groups will have inadvertently paid someone twice. This is amplified by the fact that certain vendors have been reviewing older activity and billing for items they claim were never paid for.

An added bonus of searching for duplicate payments is that the same techniques frequently will uncover fraud, another unpleasantry expected to skyrocket throughout the crisis. Again, even though your plate is full, don't skip this step.

Step 8: Review all ACH debit activity initiated throughout the emergency against your accounts. Some organizations, unable to start an ACH program in the middle of the crisis, allowed their vendors to initiate ACH debits against their accounts. If you don't wish for them to continue doing this, make sure you have an ACH block on bank accounts.

To ensure you don't also pay those vendors with a check when you return, double check those payments and make sure all associated documents (open purchase orders and receiving documents) have been extinguished.

Step 9: If you currently make ACH payments but do not have all your vendors enrolled in the program, ramp up your efforts to enroll additional vendors. Suppliers who previously turned their noses up at the thought of an electronic payment are now changing their tune. Just as accounts payable departments struggled to retrieve paper invoices and cut paper checks while working remotely, accounts receivable and treasury departments faced a similar challenge when it came to retrieving checks and getting them deposited in the bank.

And while you are working on your campaign to engage existing vendors in your ACH program, expect to hear from vendors who are accepting electronic payments. They will be looking to enroll you in their programs.

Step 10: If you are not currently making ACH payments to B2B vendors, talk to your bank about starting such a program. Banks are expecting a flood of such calls and will welcome such inquiries. But don't wait too long. Remember some experts are predicting another outbreak of coronavirus next winter. Hopefully, they are wrong. But we need to be prepared if they are not.

Once you have lined up your bank, you will need to start an outreach effort to your vendors. You might start with any who have contacted your organization with a request that you pay them electronically. Not only will they not need their hands held through the process, they will be more understanding of an y snafus you might run into.

Step 11: If your organization has had layoffs, cancel with the bank the cards for those employees who have been terminated. The most important step in this process is notifying the financial institution that the card has been cancelled. Given the chaos which many companies found themselves dealing with as they hurried to have employees shelter in place, some may not have gotten cards back from employees who they had to lay off. That is fine – as long as the cards are cancelled with the bank.

Steps Related to Travel and Events

Step 12: Review all p-card charges closely to ensure employees did not put items on cards that would not pass muster on their expense reports and that no cards were compromised. Now this is something that you should normally be doing, but it will taken on new dimensions during the crisis.

Why? Because people are working remotely and many have made purchases to accommodate their new working location. Some will be very reasonable, but a few inevitably will leave you scratching your head.

Also, make sure that you can account for all new cards that were sent out during the crisis – both to replace expiring cards and any new ones you may have requested.

Step 13: Establish guidelines for reimbursement of expenses employees incurred while quarantining. To ensure fairness, companies are advised, as soon as possible, to set guidelines on what they will reimburse and what they won't. In a perfect world, this would have been done before quarantine, but given the short notice, few if any had time to take this action.

Some organizations have given employees a small allowance ($100 or $250 each) and have told them not to submit incidental expenses for setting up at home. The idea being that the allowance would cover these items.

Step 14: Track all refunds for events (conferences, seminars, etc.) to ensure the organization gets them all. Many events offered to move registrations to the organization's next event. Some of your employees may have decided to take advantage of those offers rather than take a refund. It will be necessary to track those new registrations to make sure they are used. If they are not, the company will be entitled to a refund.

The event fee is not the only expense that must be refunded or tracked. Some had prepaid hotel rooms and of course, many had booked airfare. These can be tricky as some of the service providers urged their customers to take credits for future use. So, this too should be tracked. It goes without saying that this will create more work for the staff that administers your expense reimbursement programs. Payments that were made with credit cards will be credited back to the card used originally to make the payment. Some will end up with credit balances on their cards. Make sure this is accounted for correctly.

Step 15: As many reading this are aware it is a recommended best practice that employees use the corporate card for all travel expenses, if the organization has a card program. Yet almost half of all organizations still allow employees to use personnel cards, if they so choose. This will make the chore of monitoring refunds infinitely more difficult. Refunds that went directly to employees' credit cards now need to be remitted to employer. More than a few employees may "forget" to turn the refunds back to their organization.

Complicating this issue even further are the cases where a refund was put on a card of an employee who has been terminated, perhaps due to business downturn caused by COVID-19. Getting the refund back from this employee will not be easy, if they do not choose to voluntarily turn it over.

Step 16: Many organizations will want to establish interim travel policy. They may feel there are safety considerations, there may be financial belt tightening or they may feel everyone needs to stay put and work on getting the organization up and running. This shouldn't be overly difficult when it comes to conferences and seminars because most have been canceled at least for the next few months. The fall will be a different story.

So, just as with reimbursing expenses, setting a uniform travel policy will ensure fairness to all employees. It will also be of great help to the staff tasked with evaluating reimbursement requests. It will give them the authority they need to either pay or reject a reimbursement request.

Step 17: Some organizations that are closed are not receiving mail. The post office is returning mail, including any checks you may have sent them for payment. These will have to be reconciled upon the return to the office and possibly reissued.

But rather than reissue, take this opportunity to contact the vendor and ask if they will accept electronic payments. Before reissuing the payment, double check to make sure you have not already paid them.

Steps Related to Other AP Issues

Step 18: Review the work process that was used while working remotely to make sure it was functionality adequate. Some companies, for control purposes, prevent anything in their ERP system from being printed off premise. This created problems for accounts payable organizations that normally print and file certain documents.

If this printing is being done for a state or Federal compliance issue, check with the appropriate authorities to see if the rules have been changed or are likely to change in the near future. We suspect there will be many changes. Other tasks were either skipped or not done completely. Hopefully someone on your team was keeping track of them so someone can make sure that now that things are starting to return to normal (whatever that will be) they can be addressed.

Step 19: A review of the accounts payable tech policies, especially as they relate to security is definitely in order. If you can find someone in IT with time to come down and review what was done, that would be advisable. You will also want to determine if security was adequate and identify what steps need to be taken in the future to strengthen the security protocol around the accounts payable function.

If your organization is reviewing security on a company-wide basis and coming up with guidelines for remote working make sure accounts payable abides by them. It is all too easy to decide that the protocols are clumsy and require too much effort. Don't do that.

Step 20: Consider requiring everyone in accounts payable to update their passwords on all work-related applications. Is this overkill? Perhaps, but better to be safe than sorry and this tactic costs absolutely nothing. Many, while working from home, may have been on networks that were not secure, shared computers with others who did not observe strong fraud deterrent practices or encountered other potential security-breeching issues.

This might be a good time to remind everyone of some of the tenets of a strong password (don't use your birthday etc.). Don't use your children's names strung together, the date you got married etc. They should be long, contain small and capital letters, numbers and special symbols. Each one should be different. By the way, this probably means you are going to have to write them down. In an ideal world (where none of us reside), you'd memorize them all. But as has been made painfully aware to all of us over the last two months, we live in an imperfect world. So, write them down and store the paper somewhere safe – but not so safe, you forget where you put it. (Welcome to my world).

Step 21: Conduct a payment audit. You can do this yourself or bring in a third party do handle it. Generally speaking, AP Now advises organizations to do it themselves first and then bring in a third party. The reason for doing it yourself first is to find the duplicate and erroneous payments that are easy to find yourself. The reason we are so adamant about this given what has happened is that we strongly believe there will be quite a few invoices that, despite the best efforts of the remote-working staff, will get paid twice. The goal here is to get the money back.

If you normally conduct these audits, this time around it should be more rigorous than normal. Start by requesting statements and do a thorough audit of all credits. Do not skip this step because your staff is so overworked. If you don't have the resources, simply outsource the task to a company that works completely on a contingency basis.

Step 22: Looking forward, if you have to do US tax reporting and you have not already done so, get started on your 1099 IT setup. There are two new forms for reporting that will have to be done in January 2021. If you do not know where you ERP stands on updates for this issue, call them. You cannot afford to wait on this issue.

If the virus returns in the winter, as some expect, and we have to quarantine again, and you have to do all the 1099 system updates remotely, the situation will be extremely ugly and stressful. So, while it may have been good advice three months ago, the advice is 10 times more important in the current environment.

Step 23: Some companies started dynamic discount programs during the crisis as a way to speed up payments to struggling suppliers. If your company did so, you might want to investigate whether or not you want to expand that program.

Step 24: Review your remote worker policy and processes. This needs to be coordinated with your HR department and the overall company policy. AP Now fully expects that many companies will change their stance on this issue. We've heard from several companies that are already investigating how they can eliminate some of their expensive real estate by having some employees work remotely. Make sure whatever policy you come up with for your accounts payable team conforms to company policy. Some mangers may not like remote working. They will find themselves in hot water with HR if they try and prevent their staff from working remotely, if company policy advocates for it.

What we have learned the hard way this time is that most were not prepared to work remotely – both from a process standpoint as well as a technology position. By requiring that everyone work from home at least one day a month, we can ensure that the technology will not be an issue, should this happen again. That would help relieve the stress, if this happens again.

It doesn't really address the process issue since many who currently work remotely one day a week, allocate their work or prepare for the one day when they are in the office. So, there are still some loose ends that need to be addressed and we should do that now. By taking some of the steps in Part 1 of this article (appearing last month), some of the process issue should be alleviated. But this is something we all need to think about and prepare for.

Managers and staffers who do not like part-time remote working will need to adjust to it. It is just the new normal.

Step 25: Don't forget to thank the staff who went above and beyond what was required to keep your organizations accounts payable function operational. We heard stories from numerous companies about how responsible accounts payable professionals did what needed to be done, often under very trying circumstances. Let's not forget to thank them and acknowledge their hard efforts. Last month's Tips section had some suggestions on what managers might do to let their staff know they appreciate them.

Concluding Thoughts

Miraculously, you made it through. Every organization must prepare, for this will happen in some form again. And when it does, there will be no excuse for NOT being prepared!

Chapter 2: Remote Working: The New Workplace

About 16 months before the COVID-19 crisis hit, I was running an accounts payable seminar for a group of managers. I asked the group about staff working from home and was surprised by the response. In the past whenever this issue was raised, the response was overwhelmingly negative, with nary a soul being receptive to the concept. This time, everyone in the group, had some remote workers. What's more, is they all had a positive experience with it. Some were looking to expand their efforts in this regard. They spoke of higher throughput, improved morale and lower turnover.

This was the genesis for a survey completed at that time. We wanted to see if I had encountered an isolated group of forward-thinking individuals or this was a growing trend. Another words, we wanted to determine if remote workers in accounts payable is a pipe dream or the wave of the future. To that end we surveyed close to 300 controllers, accounting managers and accounts payable managers and directors to get their read on the issue of workers in accounts payable working remotely. Let's see what we discovered.

2019 Remote Workers in AP Practices

We began by inquiring about their organization's current practices regarding remote workers. Turns out that we had a pretty progressive group at the seminar. While the larger group did not embrace the concept, the resistance was not nearly as strong as in the past. While 56% don't allow it at all, except for an occasional emergency, over one-third now have some formal program for at least part-time remote working.

The graph below shows the breakout, according to policy. One of those who did not allow remote working except for bad weather noted that "It's disingenuous to expect employees to work remotely during inclement weather but not allow them to do so regularly."

Remote Workers in AP: Current Practices

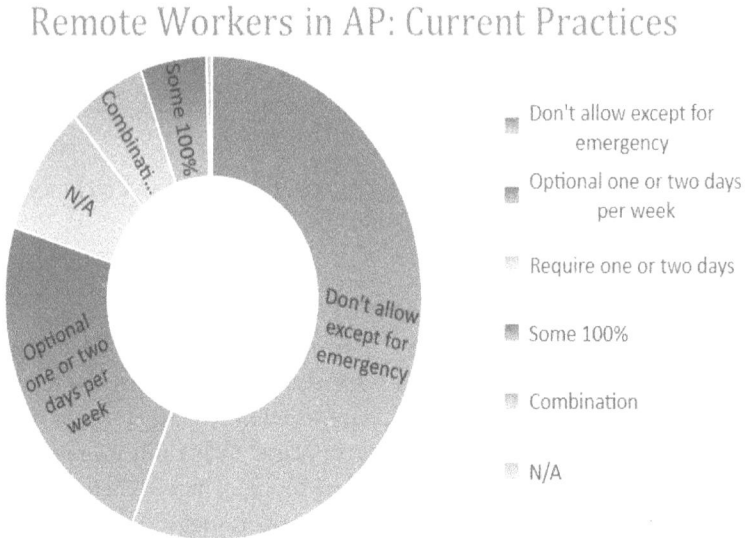

Figure 2-1 Remote Workers in AP in late 2018

Why Companies Didn't Permit Remote Workers in Late 2018

We then investigated why companies weren't allowing remote workers. Interestingly, the main reason (41%) said it was against company policy while another 37% indicated they weren't sure. What this seems to indicate is that the issue hasn't been raised and if management did discuss it, the number of companies permitting employees to work remotely would increase. As you will see as you read further on in this report, there are a number of very good reasons why companies are now actively considering changing this policy.

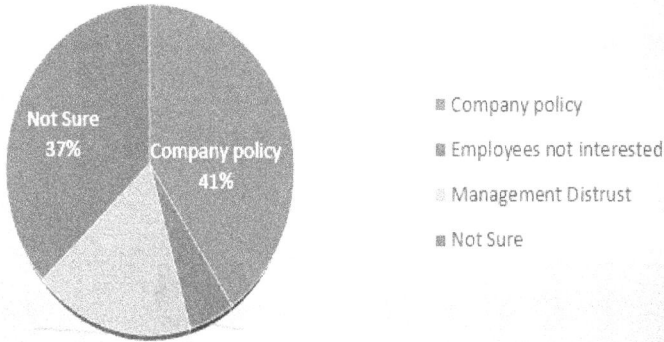

Figure 2.2 Why Companies Did Not Permit Remote Workers in AP in late 2018

Benefits

We surveyed on what we thought were the primary benefits, specifically, higher morale and coverage in bad weather. Three times as many organizations focused on the higher morale. Perhaps the biggest surprise was the number of survey respondents who wrote in that they had experienced higher productivity once they started allowing remote workers.

They also spelled out other benefits including:

- The ability to keep qualified workers who were moving
- People working longer hours because they weren't wasting time commuting
- Employees who valued the flexibility remote working offers
- Allows for lower coverage during holiday periods
- Allows employees to work on days they would have previously had to take off thus reducing the strain on others who are in the office and would have to cover for them
- Less chit-chat
- Less space needed, saving organization on costly rents

- Traffic has gotten terrible in certain cities (Atlanta, Seattle and Portland OR were mentioned several times.)
- Elevates employees to a higher sense of conscientiousness
- Very motivated employees
- Increased engagement
- Employees are more willing to work extra hours since they don't have commute time
- Turnover is almost non-existent
- Bumps up morale

We noted at the time that as the employment situation improves (good news), offering the ability to work remotely, at least part of the time, might help attract more qualified candidates. Several folks mentioned that they had not been able to hire certain sought-after candidates because of the organization's inflexibility on this issue!

Of course, those companies that had employees working remotely even occasionally had a huge advantage when the crisis hit. Their staffs had the technology in place to get started working. They were not a drain on the already overworked IT help desks. The staff on those desks were trying to get almost the whole company set up to work remotely, sometimes in as little as 48 hours. This is not to say there weren't procedural issues, but at least the technology worked.

When conducting one of the weekly AP Isolation webinars, AP Now co-hosted with the AP Association at the beginning of the crisis, we asked about the number of hours worked when isolating as compared to before isolation. Interestingly, 46% said they were working more hours. Some of that could be attributed to the fact that many people indicated the technology at home was not nearly as good as the technology in the office.

Equally interesting was the 27% who indicated that they had worked more hours initially but were back to their normal work week. Much of that can be attributed to the time needed to get the technology up and running at home.

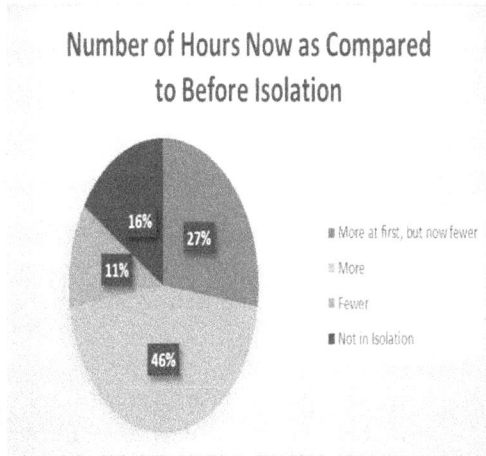

Figure 2-3 Hours worked when isolating as compared to in the office

Disadvantages

The primary disadvantage, mentioned by 12% of the applicable respondents, was that they weren't able to reach employees when they needed them. Other issues (most of which can be addressed with a little planning) included:

- Inability to deal with a Rush invoice
- Staying on top of it to make sure we are paying workers for all their hours. Some will work later and at odd times as they take more ownership for the work
- Some shuffling of workflow to accommodate the remote workers inability to deal with "paper".
- Hard to include all of the team for impromptu meetings
- Technology costs (providing laptops to those working remotely)
- Lower morale for the greater organization (jealousies, when inconsistent policies extended or with those that can't take advantage of it as regularly as others.

Interestingly, even though a few mentioned the cost issue, it was not a concern for most.

When discussing the negatives surrounding remote workers one respondent noted, "while it slows down the process once in a while, the benefits outweigh the negatives." And we saw the same thing in the comments. The number of folks commenting on advantages was far greater the handful who discussed disadvantages.

The Cost Issue

During several sessions and conversations, the issue of whether employees would be reimbursed for their Internet connection costs. There are several views on this matter. No consensus has emerged. Here are the different approaches being used:

- Some companies have given all employees working from home a small one-time stipend to cover the costs of setting up at home. These tended to be about $250
- Some companies have given employees a small monthly amount to contribute to the additional costs the employees may have to make. This tends to be about $100 per month.
- Other companies take the view that the employee is saving on commuting costs and this should more than offset the slightly higher costs of working from home. In many cases, the employee is already paying for Internet so there is no additional cost, although some may look to upgrade their service.

Just as there is a divergence in policy, employees' attitudes towards this issue vary. Some feel strongly that their companies should contribute while others are thrilled at the prospect of working from home and are more than happy to eat any small incremental costs.

Looking Forward in 2019

About 10% of those participating in the survey indicated that it was likely their organization would change their No Remote Working policy in the near future. The graph below shows the breakdown of the responses when asked about changing their minds.

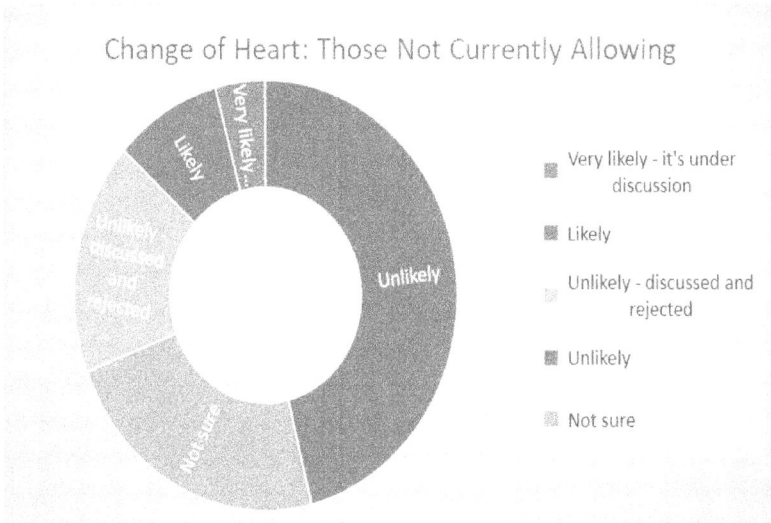

Figure 2-4 Expected Change in Remote Working Policy in late 2018

New Recommended Best Practice in 2020

Oh, what a difference a crisis can make. One of the many amazing things about this crisis is the way accounts payable teams everywhere rose to the occasion and kept their companies running. They managed to get the invoices and get them paid even though they weren't set up to do so.

More than one controller has a new-found respect for their teams in accounts payable. What's more, many are downright surprised to learn that the staff's they thought couldn't be trusted to work remotely, have shown that fear to be unwarranted.

They've also learned that paper is not a good thing and it's time to change. The move towards certain practices in accounts payable (electronic payments, remote working and even invoice automation) got accelerated with progress that might have been taken many years in the old scenario, now happening in a few short months.

New Best Practice: Everyone in accounts payable should be required to work remotely at least one day a month, but preferably one day a week. This will enable you to eliminate all the technology-related problems encountered this time. A few of your employees won't like this as they don't like working remotely. That's fine but they should do it at least once a month.

In all likelihood, during the next few years the workplace will evolve into something that is very different than what we have today. There will be more remote workers not only as companies come to trust their employees but as they also look to reap the financial rewards of having less office space and a larger remote staff.

Don't Overlook the Morale Issue

During one of our AP Isolation events, we asked folks what they missed the most from their old office life. The answer might surprise you. What attendees missed the most was not the better technology at work (although many did miss that) but their co-workers. It headed the list. Many missed someone to chat over coffee, at lunch or just for a few minutes at the proverbial water cooler. The graph below shows their responses.

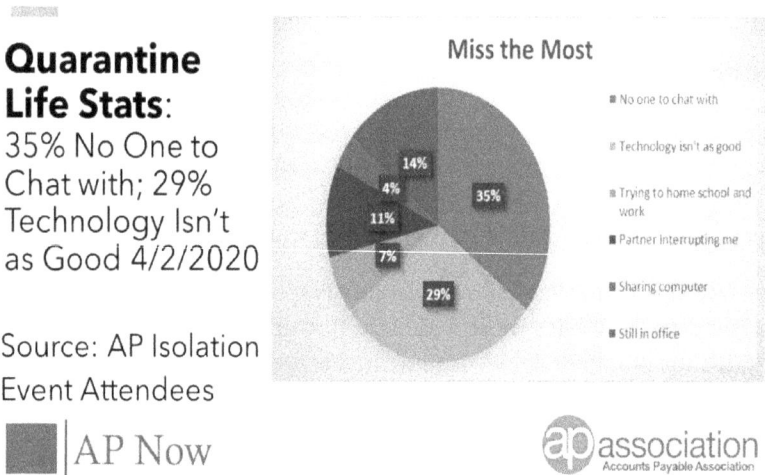

Figure 2-5 What Employees Missed the Most during Quarantine

Even more surprising, when asked to identify the technology they missed the most, many took the opportunity to write "their co-workers."

Quarantine Life Stats:
Technology
Missed the Most
4/21/2020

Most missed: Two Screens
Second most: Internet (speed)
Most (Write In): Co-Worker

Source: AP Isolation
Event Attendees

AP Now

association
Accounts Payable Association

Figure 2-6 Technology Missed the Most

The dual screens topped this list of what they accounts payable staff missed the most. Lack of two screens was probably influential in requiring some to work more hours than when they were in the office, as dual screens makes keying invoices easier.

The emphasis on missing their co-workers brings up another point, that should not be overlooked if working remotely for long periods of time. That is the need to ensure you keep morale up and in contact, so they don't feel out of the loop and as though they don't belong to the group.

Tips on Improving AP Staff Morale and Showing Appreciation

It's been a rough four to six weeks for most accounts payable groups. They've either had to go into quarantine with little notice or were designated essential personnel and are going into the office most days.

If they are isolating, they are often dealing with less-than-perfect technology, working in less-than-ideal circumstances (space, homeschooling, being alone etc.) while trying to get their work done. What has emerged is the number one thing most miss from their old work process are their peers.

At the same time those who continue to go into the office also are finding new challenges. It can be more difficult to get in touch with vendors, often there is only a skeleton staff and that can be a little unnerving, and often times the only lunch options are what you remembered to bring from home.

Regardless of the situation during the current crisis, almost every accounts payable team will benefit from some morale boosters and/or acknowledgement and appreciation of their efforts. Here are some tactics you might employ.

1. AP Now is joining our colleagues across the pond, the AP Association, in celebrating AP Appreciation Week, which runs from May 18-22. We hope you'll join us in planning some fun for the week, even though we suspect many will still be working from home. If you miss this, check back for next year.

2. Plan weekly (or more frequent) online staff meetings, making sure to reserve plenty of time to for staffers to share what's going on in their personal lives. One expert has suggested that first thing Monday morning is NOT the ideal time for these get togethers. If you can use Zoom or some other technology that allows members to see each other, all the better.

3. Share pictures on Slack, maybe pets or crazy hats, something that everyone can participate in. Some companies have had success during this crisis encouraging employees to share photos demonstrating their hobbies.

4. Run an occasional silly contest or online game that everyone can participate in. The five-minute bucket list during an online meeting might provide a lot of laughs.

5. If you are using Slack, Donut is a Slack extension that randomly pairs up team members for a non-work-related conversation.

6. Run a recipe roundup, with each staff member contributing one of their favorite recipes.

7. Play the icebreaker challenge. Each person shares one little-known fact about themselves. If you have more than five or six team members, these can be submitted to the manager ahead of time. These can be shared online at the beginning of a meeting and each staff member gets to guess which fact belongs with which person. The person who gets the most correct wins the prize. If the staff is small, then they can each share this fact with the others at the start

of a team meeting. A similar contest can be run with everyone submitting a baby picture.

8. Try virtual karaoke at the beginning of a team meeting. You can either pick a song you are sure everyone knows or provide the written lyrics ahead of time.

9. Start a game of "You Are Awesome." It can be run on a Slack channel or with an email thread. Here's how it works. Any team member can give shout-outs to other team members. Once it's started everyone else chimes in adding emojis to the chain.

10. Saying thank you for all their hard efforts will go a long way. Sometimes, we're all working so hard that we forget to stop and let our staff know that their efforts are appreciated.

Tips on Making Remote Working Work

As alluded to earlier, one of the crucial factors in having a successful remote worker policy is pre-planning. By anticipating where you might run into problems, you can plan around them. What follows are some tips shared by survey participants successfully running such programs.

- Use of metrics to track productivity is critical, if you must show progress to management. Those who have good processes in place to do this, as well as those who have automated their invoice processing, are advised to regularly share these analytics. It's the fastest way to prove the success of a program and to convert more naysayers. This is especially important if you have a manager who doesn't trust staff and believes everyone will goof off if not under his or her watchful eye. They be surprised when they see that productivity actually improves

- If staff is allowed to work remotely only part time, pick one day (say Wednesdays) when everyone must be in the office. Then schedule meetings for those days.

- Use a buddy system to cover for those working remotely. To ensure there's opportunity for face to face collaboration, pick one non-changing non-remote day where everyone is onsite.

- Take full advantage of Skype or Zoom and other low or no-cost communication methodologies.

- Please note that in those organizations where invoice processing is not automated, invoices rarely leave the premises. Typically, invoices are scanned and the originals stay on the premises

Two Caveats

Be aware that should you mandate partial remote working for everyone on staff, there will be a small minority who do not like it. They may live alone of be distrustful. The first is the employee who perhaps lives alone or in small quarters and relies heavily (even though they probably won't admit it) on co-workers for socialization. If you recognize this and take a few extra steps with this individual you may be able to get them to see the light. The extra step can be something as simple as scheduling a group coffee video chat or a one-on-one chat.

If you have staffers who no matter what the new technology, process or change is, they throw up roadblocks, you will need to address the matter. But, at the end of the day, one member of staff does not determine how the whole department operates.

The next problematic employee is the manager who doesn't want to remote work either for personal reasons or because they don't trust the staff. If the organization mandates a certain amount of remote working, this manager should not be allowed to prohibit his or her staff from participating in the program. It many be necessary to get HR involved to deal with this matter.

Concluding Thoughts

There has definitely been a shift in the mindset regarding this issue. The COVID-19 situation fast-tracked that. No longer do you hear great disdain around the issue. As other departments start to allow remote workers and companies experience the benefits, it is no longer considered taboo. "I expect this will become the norm more and more, especially when employers need to compete for talent," explains one of the respondents summing up the view held by a number of other survey participants.

Employees hate that they can't work from home, adds a regional controller. "Upper Management won't listen and it is hurting the recruitment of new people and the retention of younger workers," he adds.

As you can see from the comments already, worker retention is a critical issue as the economy improves. Another manager explains why his organization is considering making the leap. "We are in an area with a lot of traffic congestion, we are starting to consider this as an option, in order to retain good workers."

We allow the staff to work at home one day per week and it has had a very positive impact on our organization, says another. "You can't always give more money, but work at home is a benefit all employees enjoy and it helps morale," she concludes.

Our Conclusion: Remote working for an AP staff is definitely the wave of the future, for a good chunk of the workforce. And as an added benefit, much of the staff who work in accounts payable actually love working remotely one or two days a week

CHAPTER 3: THE CURRENT STATE OF INVOICE PROCESSING

In early 2020 before the COVID-19 crisis, AP Now conducted an invoice survey co-sponsored by Nacha, the group that administers electronic payments through the ACH (such as direct deposit of payroll and direct payments to vendors). The results paint a picture of current practices and what they portended for the future – before it became patently clear what a royal pain paper invoices are.

Common Invoice Formats

Unsurprisingly, the most common, but definitely not only, method for receiving invoices is email, with almost 100% receiving invoices this way. That being said, there are still many invoices being received through the post. The advent of the coronavirus crisis and many AP operations working remotely has highlighted just how beneficial email or portal receipt of invoices is. One of the most common concerns of AP staffs working remotely was how to get invoices mailed to the organization.

The most common format for invoices; PDF. Word files and spreadsheets also widely used, with half of the respondents receiving invoices in each of these other formats. Alas, the most common handling practice of emailed invoices (60%) is to print them out and enter the data manually. This is definitely NOT a best practice!

If automation is not used, getting two screens and teaching processors to key from one is the recommended approach. This is not to say that invoices will never be printed. Occasionally, there will be a need and that is acceptable.

Horrifically, the problem of duplicate submission of invoices continues to hound almost all AP departments, with over 80% indicating they have this issue and they receive multiple copies of about 16% of their invoices.

Every organization should develop practices that discourage suppliers from sending more than one copy of a particular invoice before the due date. This creates a ton of extra work in the accounts payable department and occasionally one of those duplicates gets through.

While use of a vendor portal would annihilate this menace, portals are not used as often as one think. Despite the fact that a huge number of companies have purchased these solutions, use of the portals in many organizations is lackluster at best. The lack of use of vendor portals is due to a number of factors, among them the AP staff sometimes encourages vendors to send paper or email. Others say they haven't received adequate training while still others claim they are difficult.

Some of this can be attributed to portals that require vendors visit it to submit their invoices, but that is only a small part. The often-unspoken issue is that processors are sometimes concerned that the portals will eliminate their jobs. This is compounded when training is inadequate.

Finally, despite all the technology and for a variety of reasons discussed above, about 80% of all invoices still entered manually. This despite the fact that almost three-quarters have paid for some sort of an invoice automation solution. As discussed above, usage of these at many organizations is less than ideal. Those who have put the money and time into purchasing these solutions must find a way to make better use of them.

What's Going Away

In reviewing the data from these surveys as well as talking to several experts in the field, it became obvious that several things are not taking off the way their creators would have liked. In all probability, they will not survive. Hence, it is probably not a good idea to rely on them for future innovation. Let's take a look at three of them.

Issue #1: Third-party master vendor file portals have not seen wide-spread adoption. While these portals are very attractive to the accounts payable community, the vendor community is not enthralled. In fact, there are few topics that can raise the hackles of a credit or accounts receivable professional faster than this issue—unless of course, you look at the next two issues. The surveys reveal that almost 85% house their master vendor file in their ERP. This is a huge hurdle, even if everything else were in place. Others house the information in a separate file, such as Excel. At the end of the day there is very little usage of third-party portals. In all likelihood, the third-party, master vendor files on steroids will disappear. ☹

Issue #2: Invoice portals that require vendors visit the portal to deliver the invoice or enter invoice information are also not popular. And to be fair, it is easy to see why the supplier community is not enchanted with them. They create a ton of extra work for the supplier, with no corresponding benefit. Of the handful that have such portals, only a small portion of invoices are received through it. Expect these types of portals to either adapt or die.

Issue #3: Invoice portal that charge the supplier to submit invoices. The number is extremely small (less than 5%) and usage is dismal. AP Now expects this practice to also disappear.

How the Receipt of an Invoice Can Cause Problems

Once the accounts payable staff began working remotely, the problems of receiving invoices through the mail became quite clear. Before the crisis, when AP Now surveyed its members and readers, it discovered that while most were received electronically, there were still a large number coming in through the postal mail.

The chart below shows how companies were receiving invoices. When looking at the total volume, a whopping 27% were still paper. The chart below shows the usage of the different types of delivery mechanisms.

How Invoices are Received

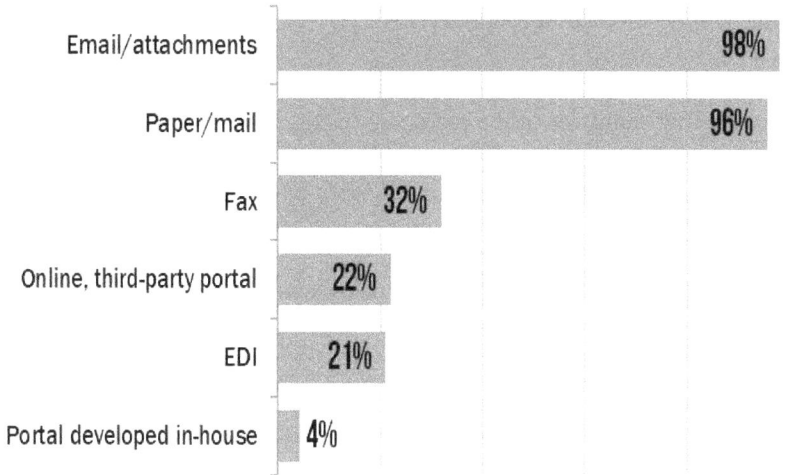

Email/attachments	98%
Paper/mail	96%
Fax	32%
Online, third-party portal	22%
EDI	21%
Portal developed in-house	4%

Figure 3-1: How Invoices Are Received

New Best Practice: All invoices should be received through via an electronic delivery mechanism, either portal (invoice automation) or email. Do not interpret this as a mandate that says if you don't use invoice automation you are not using best practices. That is not what we are saying. What we are saying is that you need to receive invoices in a manner that will allow you to access them remotely, regardless of the reason.

3 Practices that will Facilitate Best Practice Invoice Receipt

To ensure timely receipt of all invoices, implement the following tactics:

1. Set up a dedicated fax line to receive faxed invoices. It should be married to an e-fax functionality so each fax is converted to an electronic document and emailed.

2. Set up a separate e-mail account for the receipt of invoices. It should only be used for the receipt of invoices and not for personal e-mail. The address should be something like invoices@abccompany.com not a personal e-mail address. Someone should be assigned to check the accounts several times a day. When the person assigned that task is out of the office, the responsibility should go to someone else just as opening the mail would be.

3. Write up instructions for your welcome packet that includes directions on how to fax or e-mail invoices. This information should also be distributed to current vendors. Suggest to them that it is not in their best interest to send invoices through the mail.

Why Invoice Portals Are Not Being Used. One of the most startling revelations that came out of the recent invoicing survey was that 80% of all invoices are still being entered manually. Why is this happening when approximately 70% of those surveyed say they have some form of invoice automation. Here are the most common reasons given:

- Most common reason (19% of respondents): AP staff encourages vendors to send paper or emailed invoices instead of using the portal.
- Lack of training was the second most common reason provided, with almost 10% citing that as the reason they believe portals aren't utilized more.
- The third most common reason given was the claim that the portals are not easy to use.

Additional reasons provided include:

- Many invoices are submitted via interfaces. We also have 8 ERP systems where Invoicing Portal is not offered for all. Also working on rolling this out Internationally for better participation
- Staff has no desire to have an invoice portal
- Vendors send invoices in the wrong format (excel or word instead of pdf) and the invoice gets rejected; duplicate invoices get sent to the system
- Small vendors do not usually participate

Clearly, training can be improved and is the easiest solution. That would probably also reduce the number of people saying that the portals are difficult to use. But, the fear that staff has that using portals will lead to the elimination of their jobs also needs to be addressed.

The Winning Invoice Automation Solution

If you are looking for a new invoice automation solution or to replace an existing one, here are some features you should require:

Feature #1: The solution does not require the vendor to do anything special, such as upload invoices into a special portal, pay a fee or anything the supplier wouldn't normally do.

Feature #2: The solution should have to go into email and pull emails with invoices attached and scrape the information without any human intervention.

Feature #3: The solution ideally should provide status information to the supplier, i.e. notification of receipt of invoices and estimated payment date. This feature should be automated or be included in an online portal that the vendor can check, if they wish. The notification of the receipt of the invoice can be in the online portal or can be an automated email sent upon receipt of the invoice.

Concluding Thoughts

Invoice processing has been changing for some time. Automation has been making parts of it easier and more efficient. That trend continues. We expect that as time goes on, companies not using one of these solutions will be the exception rather than the rule. The professionals who figure out not only how to use these solutions but also how to pull additional productivity and management reporting from them will be the winners.

Invoices Missing Information

The COVID-19 crisis amplified the issue of invoices without complete information. Part of the reason for this is that communication with vendors, in many cases, became more difficult. One of the most aggravation problems facing the accounts payable team is those invoices missing the purchase order (PO) number and/or the name of the person who placed the order. How is the person processing the item supposed to get the approval to pay if they don't know who to get it from? This problem can and should be nipped in the bud.

The natural tendency is for AP to try and figure out who these invoices should be sent to for approval, which is what more than half of the respondents do (57%). However, this is not the best practice, as it does not address the underlying issue.

Other Approaches Used: In AP Now's Internal Controls in AP Survey, respondents identified a number of approaches they took when faced with this problem. Without exception, they all added time and utilized resources that could be better spend doing other tasks. Here are some of them:

- Return to supplier or department depending on who sent to us.

- Try to determine who they should go to and contact vendor to request the missing information.

- Given to purchasing to research.

- A combination of the clerk requesting the PO from vendor or the business owner.

- Invoices are directed to the person ordering the goods or services and they are responsible for indicating the payment process.

- Contact vendor for information regarding the order.

- Images are sent to purchasing for them to work with vendor.

- Contact the vendor for proof of delivery.

- We enter them in our system coding to an accrual account and place the voucher on hold until our Purchasing Dept identifies the PO to use for us. This allows us to accrue the expense and have a record of it in the system for inquiries.

- Return to the purchasing unit.

- Direct to the appropriate Buyer to research the PO.

- We call or e-mail the vendor asking who ordered the item.

As you can see, while all these techniques will work, they require added efforts and time in order to get the invoice paid. But is this really necessary? Is there a better way?

Best Practice: Vendors will continue to send such invoices unless the organization consistently returns them to the applicable vendors, requesting the missing information. Almost one-fourth (24%) of respondents take this action. AP Now believes 100% of all organizations should be using this approach. As you can see from the numbers, there's a lot of progress to be made in this area. It's time for all organizations not utilizing this approach to consider making the change. It will eliminate quite a bit of non-value add work.

We have talked with two organizations who rigorously use this method and they both report that within a short period of time all their vendors submit invoices with all the information needed to pay them. Vendors want to be paid and they want to be paid as quickly as possible. By letting them know what information you need on their invoices, you help them achieve that goal. As long as you are polite about your request, perhaps wording the request in terms of WIIFT (what's in it for them), no one should be offended.

The WIIFT is that they will be paid more quickly if you don't have to waste time trying to figure out who needs to approve the payment. So, truly, while it might not seem like it at first glance, this can be a win-win for everyone involved.

Handling Invoice Copies with a Different Invoice Number

Like invoices missing information, the problem of second invoices with a different invoice number is more difficult to address during a crisis. But this doesn't mean we shouldn't. Second invoices with a different invoice present a unique challenge for the organization trying to avoid making duplicate payments. For starters, this is just one more issue that highlights the fact that you cannot rely 100% on the invoice number to identify a potential duplicate. Therefore, duplicate payment identification routines must rely on more than the invoice number. Here are some tactics that will help.

- 1 – Follow best practices for invoice processing is probably the single best tactic you can use to combat this nasty problem. These include using rigid coding standards, the three-way match and immediate extinguishing of the purchase order and receiving document when the payment is scheduled.
- 2 – As soon as you identify vendors who use a different invoice number, add them to the small list of vendors whose invoices are double checked.
- 3 – You can try talking to the vendor and asking them to use the original invoice number but don't expect this to be overly successful. At the end of the day, the vendor will have established practices and it is not likely you will be able to change them.

Some believe that vendors who use this approach do so purposely to try and get some of their customers to pay twice. You will never be able to prove or disprove this theory. So, your best defense is to follow best practices and make sure you are not one of their customers who double pays.

When Best Practices Are Lacking: Advice on Improving Controls during a Crisis

Best practices exist for a reason. In the accounts payable function, they tighten controls, help thwart fraud and duplicate payments and basically allow the function to run as efficiently as possible. That being said, the recently-conducted AP Practices survey reveals surprisingly low usage of best practices in the real world. In fact, when measuring utilization of seven common best practices, we did not find one organization using them all although we did find a number who had integrated none of them into their processes. Of the seven practices studied, companies used, on average, just three.

Let's take a look at the utilization of common best practices and include suggestions on how the situation can be improved at organizations where the best practice in question is not in use.

1. **Best Practice**: Mandatory use of an Invoice Coding Standards and checking regularly to make sure processors are using it.
   Usage: 54% Another 25% said they have a coding standard and believe it is being used but don't check.
   Comment: This is one of the best protections against making a duplicate payment and it costs nothing to do. There is really no excuse for not doing it. Of course, if invoice automation ever becomes widespread, this issue will go away.
   Suggestion: The checking to make sure processors are using the coding standard does not have to be very time consuming. Randomly and on a surprise basis, sit with a processor for 30 minutes and watch them process or pull a few invoices they entered and see if their coding matches the standard.

2. **Best Practice**: Mandatory use of a Coding Standard when entering data in the master vendor file and checking regularly to make sure the coding standard is being used.
   Usage: 59% with another 27% believing it is being used but not verifying.
   Comment: Again, this approach helps protect against fraud and duplicate payments. This no-cost technique guards against duplicate entries in the file for the same vendor.

Suggestion: Verification can be done sporadically for short periods of time. The same standard can be used for invoice coding and data entry in the master vendor file.

3. **Best Practice**: Email invoices should be directed to a separate email address set up to receive invoices only.
    Usage: 54% although some are directing invoices to a portal.
    Comment: Since it is quite likely that email will be the primary mode of delivery for invoices in the next few years, it is critical that every organization incorporate this into their everyday practices. Of course, setting up the email account does not guarantee vendors will use it. Some will persist in sending invoices to people who they "think" will get them priority treatment.
    Suggestion: Educate your vendors that sending invoices anywhere but to the email address set up to receive invoices will only delay the processing of their invoice and hence their payment.

Chapter 4: How to Encourage/Mandate Invoices by e-Mailed

The current crisis highlighted the importance of being able to receive invoices in a manner that is not location specific, i.e. some sort of electronic delivery. While we've made great strides in receiving invoices electronically, the recent Nacha/AP Now survey conducted at the beginning of 202o revealed that 27% of invoices still come through the post. Keep in mind that in some cases the supplier is actually paying for Overnight Delivery services so the cost is even higher (for those organizations) than you might imagine.

The trick here is to convince suppliers to deliver their invoices in a manner not reliant on physical delivery. Now, it is likely that after this crisis, many relying on the post will see the light. But, we suspect, not everyone will. The task of those who deal with them is to convince them to get rid of the paper. This section is devoted to helping with that issue as well as a few other related invoice issues. Let's start with some simple tactics you might try.

Several Tactics to Increase the Number of Invoices Received Electronically

The way we receive invoices has changed dramatically in the last few years. Just a few short years ago, emailed and faxed invoices were considered a royal pain by many. Today, most organizations are looking for ways to get vendors to send invoices electronically or by fax. As regular readers of this publication are aware, faxed invoices can easily be converted to emailed invoices by using relatively inexpensive e-fax services. What follows are three simple steps every organization can use to decrease the number of invoices received in paper format.

1) Let them know you are amenable to receiving invoices electronically. As amazing as it may seem, some vendors will not realize you are set up to receive invoices electronically. Let them know. You can include a one line notice about this on all remittance advices or you can send all vendors sending invoices through the postal service a letter telling them how to send you their invoices in ways other than the mail service. You might point out the benefits they will accrue by moving to electronic delivery.

2) Make it easy for those not using a third-party system. Some vendors are not equipped or willing to participate in third party services. Provide them with a separate email address to use to send invoices. This might be something like invoices@abccompany.com or ap@abccompany.com. If you have an e-fax service don't forget to provide the fax number. If they are more comfortable faxing, let them.

3) Entice them by agreeing to pay them electronically if they invoice you electronically. This is an especially easy approach to use if you were looking to pay electronically anyway. You get two wins for the price of one effort.

4) Remind vendors that you use a FIFO (first in, first out) approach to processing invoices. So, if they email them to you, you are apt to receive them faster than if they put them in the post. During the COVID-19, some companies had an employee go into the office once a week to collect invoices and other mail. This would further delays the processing of invoices sent through the post.

5) During the crisis, some companies went 100% remote. In more than a few of these instances, the post office returned the mail that was sent to these companies. This included invoices. So, if the invoice was never received, it could not be processed.

6) If these strategies don't work, try mandating electronic delivery of invoices. While this might have been seen as a bullying tactic before the coronavirus crisis, it is likely to be seen as less threatening afterwards.

An Action Plan to Convince Vendors

Trying to stop vendors from sending invoices by e-mail is like trying to stop the water once the dam or levy has broken. Given the inevitability of e-mailed invoices, it is far better to develop an effective plan to take advantage of this new delivery method than to fight it. What follows is a rather simple seven-step process any organization can use to address the receipt of e-mailed invoices situation.

Step 1: Recognize that you can't fight the proverbial City Hall and establish a formal policy for handling e-mailed invoices. This should be part of your formal policy and procedures manual for the accounts payable function.

Step 2: Set up one e-mail address to receive invoices from suppliers. This should be part of your best practice strategy to receive all e-mails in one centralized location. Today that means one postal address, one e-mail address and one fax address. The e-mail address should not a personal address but one that can be accessed by several people. This way, if someone is unexpectedly out of the office or leaves the company, there is no disruption to vendors e-mailing invoices.

Step 3: Provide the email address established for the receipt of invoices to all suppliers. This can be done in both the Welcome Packet for new vendors and the annual letter to vendors. If you normally don't send an annual letter to vendors, you might send a special communication regarding this e-mail address.

Step 4: Vendors should be informed that only invoices should be sent to this address. Nothing else sent to that address will be forwarded to other parties.

Step 5: Vendors should be instructed not to send a second invoice by snail mail. Be aware that some will disregard this directive. Watch this process and create a list of vendors who always double submit despite your instructions. Paper invoices from these vendors should be discarded.

Step 6: Different people should be assigned to monitor the account on different days. They can also fill in for each other when someone is out or on vacations.

Step 7: Upon receipt of an invoice, it should immediately be reviewed and forwarded to the appropriate party for approval.

The Benefits Checklist

When discussing the need to submit invoices electronically, consider using the checklist below:

1. Have you pointed out to your suppliers that faster receipt of invoices means it is more likely you'll have the invoiced processed in time to pay on the due date? __ Yes __ No

2. Have you pointed out the cost savings associated with not having to print invoices? __ Yes __ No

3. Have you pointed out the cost savings associated with not having to pay for postage? __ Yes __ No

4. Have you pointed out the cost savings related to salaries of associates who won't have to manually stuff of invoices in envelopes? __ Yes __ No

5. Have you pointed that no longer will invoices be lost in the mail? __ Yes __ No

6. Have you pointed out that should the vendor lose an invoice, replacing it will be simple and inexpensive? __ Yes __ No

7. Have you reminded your suppliers that with e-invoicing there's no need to take invoices to post office? __ Yes __ No

8. Have you suggested that in the unlikely event they had to send second invoices if a customer (not you, of course) hadn't paid by due date, the process is much simpler than in a paper-based environment? __ Yes __ No

9. Have you reminded your suppliers that if and e-mail address is not good, they would be notified immediately, not two to eight weeks later when mailed invoices finally come back? __ Yes __ No

10. Have you also noted that invoices don't get damaged in the e-mail the way they occasionally do in snail mail? __ Yes __ No

Discussion of Benefits Checklist

We don't think it necessary to go through each of the items on the checklist in individual detail. We think the responses are obvious. All of the items on the checklist are benefits to the supplier sending invoices. Clearly, there are also a whole slew of benefits to the customer, as well. But the purpose of the checklist is to arm organizations who are trying to convince vendors to bill electronically so the focus is on that end only. That is why we don't discuss things like making it easier to earn early payment discounts.

The Savings Plan

Most commonly, e-mailed invoices are first turned into a PDF and then sent to the customer. Great care needs to be taken that each is only processed once. For if you print the PDF, the hundredth printing will look just as good as the first one and you won't be able to tell which is the original and which is the copy. This means that routines for weeding out duplicates are more important than ever. It should also entail duplicate payment checking routines be integrated into the invoice processing function.

Invoices that are e-mailed are a reality every organization has to deal with. Trying to avoid the issue is not smart. Following a game plan, such as the one discussed above, is your best strategy for making this new approach work for your organization.

Keep in mind that some invoices are sent either as a Word file or an Excel spreadsheet. The spreadsheet is often used when there are many different line items and this detail needs to be loaded into the ERP for processing.

The Handling of E-mailed Invoices

Electronic invoicing, or e-invoicing, means different things to different people. Some folks use the term to refer to automated invoice processing systems, usually run by third parties. But most take a more inclusive approach and use the term to include invoices e-mailed by the vendor to the customer, usually in the form of a PDF file.

Research by AP Now reveals that the vast majority of companies now receive at least a few invoices by e-mail. This growing practice puts some form of e-invoicing within the reach of virtually every organization.

Best Practice: Develop a policy for encouraging vendors who are not using third party e-invoicing systems to e-mail their invoices. This benefits not only the supplier but the customer as well. Invoices are received quickly and can be routed for approvals. If the company is using an imaging process, it saves them from the time and expense of having to do the imaging themselves.

Establish a routine for handling invoices emailed by suppliers. It might include the following:

- Set up one e-mail address to receive invoices from suppliers
- Provide this email address to suppliers, either in the Welcome Packet or annual letter to vendors.
- Vendors should be informed that only invoices should be sent to this address. Nothing else sent there will be forwarded.
- Vendors should be instructed not to send a second invoice by snail mail. Be aware that some will disregard this directive.
- The e-mail address should not be an address associated with an individual but rather one that can be access by several people
- Different people can be assigned to forward the e-mails in the account on different days and can fill in for each other when someone is out or on vacations
- Upon receipt of the invoice, it should immediately be reviewed and forwarded to the appropriate party for approval.

If you have a fax number set up to receive invoices, and you should, connect it to an e-fax facility. This will take the paper invoice, convert it to an e-mail and you'll never see a piece of paper.

Almost Best Practice: For those who still prefer the paper, and there are more than a few such companies, establish a routine similar to the one described above for handling e-mailed invoices. The reason for this is that some vendors are now refusing to mail invoices claiming it is too expensive.

Thus, whether an organization wants to or not, they are going to be forced to deal with e-mailed invoices. So, it is best to have a policy. And, those who establish a policy for vendors insistent on emailing invoices may find that they prefer this method of delivery. When that happens they will then begin to encourage all vendors to deliver invoices electronically.

Special Pointers for Accounts Payable: With the advent of the PDF invoice, as well as advances made by technology, it is now very easy to have many original looking invoices. What's more, fewer and fewer suppliers are marking the second invoices they send as Duplicate or Copy. Hence, we need to change the way we look for duplicate invoices.

What's more, with a sizeable number of suppliers both snail mail and e-mailing the same invoice, duplicate checking routines have never been more important. Stringent coding standards and standardized routines for processing invoices are important. For it is no longer possible to identify a duplicate or copied invoice simply by looking at it.

Worst Practice: Worst practices include:

- Refusing to accept e-mailed invoices
- Not establishing an e-mail address for invoices to be sent
- Allowing the use of employees' email accounts to receive invoices (and when they leave the company those invoices end up nowhere)

More Best Practices: Given that virtually every company is now receiving invoices delivered by email, it is time to look at best practices around that process. They should include:

- Set up a separate email address for the use of receiving invoices.
- Access to this separate email address should be given to several people, so invoices do not go unprocessed in cases of unexpected absences.
- Suppliers should be discouraged from sending invoices to any email address other than the special one set up for invoices.
- All suppliers, as well as all employees who may receive invoices, should be notified of this separate email address and instructed to send invoices to it, and no place else.
- Set up a protocol for the saving of invoices, if you are not using an e-invoicing module. This will ensure that when the same invoice is

received more than once, it doesn't get saved as two separate invoices.

- If you are using an e-invoicing module, set up procedures to have the emailed invoices uploaded. This may even be automated.

- Create standardized procedures for the handling of invoices received by email, ideally one that does not involve printing the invoices. It should match the process used with invoices received in the mail. This will help weed out invoices sent using both mediums.

- Vendors who send invoices more than once or to multiple parties should be contacted and given instructions on the proper submission of invoices. Do not expect them all to comply. Many are primarily interested in getting paid not in making their customers' accounts payable department more cost effective.

Special Practices for E-mailed Invoices

Suppliers should be provided with some guidelines for submitting invoices by e-mail. Here are a few best practices regarding that issue:

1.   The subject line should include a standard statement such as Invoice Attached and the PO number.

2.   Invoices should be sent to the e-mail address and nowhere else. There is no need to send copies to other parties. This just increases the chances of them being processed and possibly paid twice.

3.   Each invoice should be in a separate PDF.

4.   If there is backup documentation, that may be included in the same PDF file, although the invoice must be the first page.

5.   Each invoice should be sent in a separate e-mail.

6.   There is no need to include a cover memo or note with the invoice. The first page of the PDF file should be the invoice itself.

7.   The PDF should be sent as an attachment. Invoice information should not be pasted into the body of the e-mail message.

8.   Statements and other correspondence should not be sent to the e-mail address set up for the receipt of invoices.

Chapter 5: Starting an Invoice Automation Program

Although invoice automation has been around for over 20 years, the first models were clunky, expensive and required extensive IT involvement. Implementation was also time consuming. That is simply not the case anymore. Today's models, often with no up-front investment required, can be implemented quickly (in a matter of hours, not weeks) and do not require extensive training. They are available on a SaaS basis and are quite affordable.

To stick your head in the sand and ignore this innovation is foolish. At some point, management will become aware of it and demand the accounts payable function utilize the new technology. If you have already started using invoice automation, make sure you are utilizing all features. If you have not started yet, start researching what's available. This way you can make the recommendation to management and be seen as a forward-thinking professional who should be a key player going forward.

Critical Factors in Successful Automation Programs

- High-level management sponsorship, without which any program is almost certainly doomed to fail.

- Organizational alignment of procurement, finance (accounts payable), treasury, and IT. If one leg doesn't do its share, the whole program can collapse
- Written policies and procedures so each group knows what it is supposed to do. These policies need to be coordinated so there are no conflicts or loopholes.

An Implementation Plan

With the cost of invoice automation plummeting, a greater number of organizations have started to investigate the feasibility of going down the e-invoicing path utilizing a third-party service. What follows is a 20-step plan any group can use to help them select the vendor that best firsts their needs.

Step 1: Get preliminary approval from your boss to investigate invoice automation. This might entail writing a memo detailing the benefits to your organization as well as estimated cost savings. Alternatively, you may be able to get approval to investigate the issue simply by having a short conversation about the process. Whatever approach you select, make sure your boss is on board before you begin.

Step 2: Create a step-by-step list of your current invoice handling process. Review it carefully to make sure you have included every step.

Step 3: Review your current process to identify any extraneous tasks that you may be doing in connection with your processing that are not necessary. Before you eliminate them, discuss the practicality of doing this with all impacted parties. Some other department may need accounts payable to continue doing the task in question.

Step 4: Review your current process to identify any weaknesses you may have in internal controls and include tactics that will tighten these weaknesses in your proposed new automation scheme.

Step 5: Identify any unique issues you think your organization may have that may not be addressed by standard invoice automation solutions. Make sure these are carefully laid out when you issue your Request for Proposal (RFP). Discuss them in detail with any potential vendor.

Step 6: Review your lists of unique issues and potential problems to see if any can be eliminated. Are they really necessary or are they just one of the top executive's pet peeves? The reason for this is any special customization is likely to be expensive and timely. Eliminate as many as possible, if not all of them.

Step 7: Delineate what you think will be potential problems and make sure they are adequately addressed. These may be items that fall under the responsibility of the vendor or they may be items your organization has to address. For example, if you are going to need fewer processors, it will be up to your organization to decide who will be the excess and what their new responsibilities will be.

Step 8: Attend vendor webinars and online demos to get an idea what is out there. This is a much simpler way of surveying the field than to have numerous sales people visit your office. It also allows you to cut the cord early and easily if you decide a specific vendor doesn't meet your requirements.

Step 9: If you go to any association conventions or trade shows, visit the vendor booths in the exhibitor hall and collect all the marketing material you can. This is another painless way to weed out vendors whose products do not meet all your requirements.

Step 10: When you have all your ducks in a row on the home front, issue your RFP to all the vendors that appear to be likely providers. Make sure you set a firm due date. While you may want to be generous and accept RFPs that come in late, consider this. If they can't get the RFP in on time when they are trying to win your business, how are they likely to perform meeting deadlines once they've got it?

Step 11: Once you have all the RFPS, begin your thorough review making sure all your salient points are covered.

Step 12: If one of the RFPS contains an offer for something the others didn't (and it's something you'd like) consider asking your final candidates to submit a revised RFP with that feature. Again, give them a cut-off date.

Step 13: Once you have all your material, identify the three (or perhaps five) most likely potential invoice automation vendors and invite them in for a meeting. Few people have the time to meet with every last vendor.

Step 14: Be prepared with a list of questions to ask all the vendors. That way you get the same information from all the vendors and you limit the amount of follow up you'll have to do. Inevitably, one will offer information you didn't ask of the others and you'll have to do some follow up. But your goal should be to keep that follow-up to a minimum.

Step 15: Schedule your meetings with each of the vendors fairly close together, say completing them all in a week to ten days. Since this is likely to be a relatively small group, it should not be too difficult. If you let a significant amount of time lapse between meetings you are likely to forget something.

Step 16: Immediately following the meeting, take ten minutes to write some brief notes about your observations. These impressions are likely to be invaluable when it comes to making your final decision.

Step 17: Check references. Try to find someone who has used the vendor in question's product other than the names provided for references. They will of course give good references; the vendor wouldn't have given them, if their installation did not go smoothly. If you belong to industry groups, local chapters of professional association ask at those meetings. Alternatively, if you go to national conventions, ask at those meetings. The references you can ferret out on your own will shed greater insights than the ones offered by the vendor.

Step 18: Make your proposal to management including your reasons for selecting your main choice. Include not only the financial implications, but also the people factor, the ease you'll have with working with a potential vendor. If you've had nothing but headaches with a particular vendor during the demo and RFP process, there is no reason to expect things will get better once you hire them.

Step 19: Assuming you get the green light from management, contact the vendor and begin the process of completing a contract. If you had a strong second candidate, you might hold off from notifying them that you've gone with someone else. That way, if things fall apart during the contract phase, you still have a backup candidate.

Step 20: After a contract is signed notify the other contenders that they have not been selected. Do this as politely and kindly as you can, as there is not telling when you will need the vendor in question.
 Once the contract is signed, it's time to implement. That's when the real fun begins.

Getting Your Invoice Automation Proposal Approved: Don't Forget These Extras.

Too often, when contemplating a new project related to technology, too much emphasis is put on the cost and the ROI. While we don't mean to imply these are not important considerations, they are only part of the equation when it comes to a new invoice automation process. If your proposal is solely based on the numbers, you've only got half the ammunition you need to get your proposal accepted. There are a number of bonuses, some of them not quantifiable that probably did not figure into your original calculations. But they should be included in your proposal. Let's take a look at a few of them.

Bonus #1 The invoice number control really can work – Finally! Many ERP systems will not accept the same invoice number for the same vendor. In theory, this should protect against paying the same invoice twice. In reality, most processors know that by simply adding a space or a letter to the end of the invoice number, they can force an invoice through their process. Unfortunately, it is a common practice. With automation, this simply doesn't happen and that invoice number control really will work.

Bonus #2 Discrepant or problematic invoices no longer get "lost." In a paper-based process, invoices with problems sometimes end up at the bottom of the pile, over and over again. Even worse, after spending some time on the bottom of the pile, they occasionally migrate to a desk drawer or folder. Then it's a case of out-of-sight, out-of-mind.

When these invoices don't get paid one or two things happen. The vendor may send a second or third invoice (rarely marked copy or second invoice) and sometimes the original and the copy get paid resulting in a duplicate payment, which is not likely to be returned. The other outcome is the vendor gets annoyed at the non-payment and the relationship is tarnished. Of course, the worst-case scenario is that both outcomes result.

By automating the process, it becomes impossible to lose an invoice. Invoice aging can and should be monitored by the manager. This greater visibility will result in a faster resolution of the problem and hopefully the elimination of this issue.

Bonus #3 Fewer stupid mistakes are made. While it would be nice to think the staff never makes silly errors, the reality is everyone does from time to time. The $300 invoice gets entered as $30,000 or the reverse. These mistakes, when they are brought to management's attention tend to get blown out of proportion tarnishing image of the entire department. This is regrettable and not fair; but it is reality.

In an automated world, the opportunities to make these kinds of errors are greatly minimized. Of course, if the current trends continue— and we have no reason to expect anything different— the accounts payable staff will become more integrated in the accounting and finance chain. And, this translates into greater visibility for the group, allowing them to get credit for the contributions they make.

Bonus #4 Better control is exerted over the cash flow. With invoices being entered automatically at point of entry, so to speak, it is possible to see exactly when cash will be disbursed, without any "surprise" large disbursements disrupting cash planning. Additionally, there's less of a "surge" right before quarter end and fiscal year end cut-off dates as staff rushes to get every last invoice submitted, including those that have been waiting for approvals for weeks or months. And finally, processors no longer have the ability to sneak early payments to their favorite vendors. This results in fewer early payments and has a positive impact on the organization's cash flow.

Bonus #5 For just about every organization, early payment discounts represent their very best investment alternative. Without going through the math, the standard 2/10 net 30 translates into a rate of return of 36%. Unless you're involved in some unethical practices, it is near impossible to earn that kind of return. Thus, most organizations do everything within their power to earn every last discount. Automating the invoice processing function, makes it feasible to earn all or most of the early pay discounts offered.

Bonus #6 With fewer duplicate, improper and erroneous payments being made after automation, the likelihood is that the payment auditors will find less to recover. This is a good thing and should result in reduced audit fees. This will occur in all those organizations where the audit firm is compensated on a contingency basis, based on recoveries. While the payment auditors are not likely to be pleased with this outcome, your organization's bottom line will improve nicely.

Bonus #7 Without a doubt, invoice automation will make outsourcing look less attractive to those organizations considering this step. While few like to discuss outsourcing the accounts payable function, it is a real possibility for a small number of companies. A number of accounts payable departments have successfully offered counter proposals when their organizations were evaluating the possibility of outsourcing invoice processing. Invoice automation was instrumental in the proposals of quite a few who were able to streamline their operations so outsourcing was no longer an attractive option.

Concluding Thoughts

Many of the issues discussed above are not easily quantifiable. But this does not mean they shouldn't be included in any invoice automation proposal. In fact, they may make the difference between getting the green light to go ahead. The reason for this is simple.
If you base your proposal base entirely on ROI (return on investment), there's a decent chance you'll get turned down, even with a good ROI. This is because there are likely to be other proposals from professionals in other departments with even better ROIs fighting for the same investment dollars you are trying to get. The extra non-quantifiable bonuses could make the difference.

Mandatory e-Invoicing

While mandatory e-invoicing is becoming the norm in many parts of the world, it has yet to find its way into the US. However, that change may come sooner than many had expected. Given that countries in South

America, Europe and parts of Asia are adopting it, there has been some press calling for the same in the US.

Why would there be such a call? For starters, it would help reduce the amount of unreported income (and hence tax revenues) and many believe, help reduce certain types of fraud. Only time will tell if any politician will be brave enough to champion this cause. Remember, the proposed mandatory corporate reporting initiative a few years ago?

Setting Realistic Expectations

You've heard the advice about under promising while over delivering. When it comes to introducing or ramping up e-invoicing programs, this should be the mantra of the day. We recently spoke with two experts in this arena and both emphasized how important it is to be realistic when setting expectations, not only about what it will take to get vendors enrolled but also the IT resources that may be required. Let's take a look at a few of the stakeholders.

- *Suppliers*: What we've learned in the last few years is that often the biggest obstacle facing organizations wishing to implement e-invoicing is the conversion of suppliers. But just because it may not be as easy as you would like, doesn't mean e-invoicing is not worth the effort. Remember the ROI can be extremely attractive. Making it as easy as possible for the e-invoicing suppliers to use the process. Be prepared to put in the time and effort necessary to convert suppliers to e-invoicing. It will take some time in the beginning.

- *The IT Issue*: This is much less of a consideration than it was in the past. The complexity of the technical integration between an e-invoicing solution and the financial systems used internally has been reduced considerably. Most solutions require little or no IT involvement.

- *The AP Staff*: To get the AP staff on board you'll need to address the unspoken fear that their jobs are going to be eliminated once the new solution is implemented. Assure them this is not the case, if appropriate. Don't lie to them. Also, if you can offer an alternate career path, with a little training, that will go a long way.

If there are no reassurances, staff will often work to the detriment of the process, encouraging vendors to send paper invoices and refusing to use the new system. The second issue related to staff is to ensure they have adequate training on how to use the new process. If they are not adequately trained you could see productivity go down. This is precisely what you don't want to happen.

- *Other Employees outside AP*: If there are other employees, most likely but not limited to procurement, who will interact with the new solution, it is critical that not only do you get their buy-in to the new process but they be adequately trained. Poor or inadequate training in this regard can also derail your new technology. This is an area that is more than occasionally overlooked.

Getting the Full Benefit

Before we close, we want to point out that an automated accounts payable process does not have to be an all or nothing deal. Many start with one or two pieces and then gradually adopt other pieces. End-to-end automation solutions provide the best of all worlds for accounts payable departments. That's where they get the most return for their investment. We expect to see more companies adopting this approach in the coming years.

In Conclusion

This is not a process improvement that can be put off for a few years. There is a decent chance that we'll have a repeat of the quarantine requirements within the next few years, possibly as early as this Fall. So, if you feel that an automation project is the way to go for your accounts payable processing, do not wait.

Otherwise, you could find yourself half way through the implementation when once again, you have only a few days to transport the staff to a remote working mode. And, the next time depending on the severity of the virus, we may not have the luxury of deeming some accounts payable staffers as "essential" and thereby getting a dispensation for them to go into the office.

Chapter 6: Invoice Automation: Increasing Usage of an Existing Program

As many organizations struggled to receive and process invoices during the COVID-19 crisis, it became glaringly clear that invoice automation might have helped some of them. Companies had difficulty retrieving paper invoices that were mailed, suppliers sometimes had difficulty getting invoices into the mail and more than occasionally, mail was returned because an office was shut down. All this made delivery spotty and highlighted the difficulties with paper invoices.

Clearly, it is imperative that organizations develop protocols for invoice delivery that are not location dependent. Either email or invoice automation would meet that requirement. Yet, even at organizations that have purchased an invoice automation solution, those solutions are quite frequently only being partially used. Why is this? If you could identify the reasons for lack of use, you would be well positioned to address them and increase usage.

The data from the Nacha/AP Now survey from early 2020 reveals some of the reasons invoice automation solutions are not being used as fully as they could be. Let's take a look at some of problems and how you can address them.

Problem #1: AP staff encourages vendors not to use the solution. About 18% reported they believed this to be the issue. This is most likely due to fear of job loss or perhaps the staffer in question is not comfortable using the solution and prefers to stick with the old paper-driven processes.

Solution: Identify if this is the issue and address it appropriately. Often additional training is the answer.

Problem #2: Lack of training. Almost 10% reported they thought this was the issue.

Solution: Take a good hard look at the training each of your impacted parties was given. Do you think it was adequate? Even if you do, you might ask the staff if they would like additional training on using the solution.

Problem #3: Solution not easy to use. Almost 5% reported they thought this was the issue.

Solution: They may be right or wrong in their evaluation. This is another instance where some additional training might be the answer. However, if the solution is clunky, you might investigate to see how difficult it would be to replace it. There are many user-friendly solutions on the market today.

Other problems mentioned by survey participants included:

- Vendors send invoices in the wrong format (Excel or Word instead of PDF) and the invoice gets rejected
- Small vendors do not usually participate
- Duplicate invoices get sent to the system

If vendors are still dragging their feet about participating, you might point out that next time you may not have someone willing to go into the office and address paper invoices. While you would prefer not to threaten …

Two Birds, One Stone: Make Sure You Include These Problematic Vendors

Whether you have a smooth-running accounts payable operation or one that could use a little fine tuning, the odds are good that you have three types of vendors who create the lion's share of the problems when it comes to payments. These include:

- The vendors who complain that you pay them late;
- The vendors whose invoices contain numerous errors; and
- The vendors whose invoices offering early payment terms mysteriously end up arriving late making it difficult, if not impossible to earn those attractive discounts.

Often these invoices arrive in accounts payable late making it difficult, if not impossible, to get them paid on time. While the latter group may occasionally be sent at the last minute on purpose, the first two groups are not trying to create difficulties. Let's take a look at each group to see what you can do to convince them to move them to e-invoicing.

The Late Payment Complainers

Before engaging in an effort to fix this problem, make sure they are being paid late and not just complaining in an attempt to be paid early. Once you've crossed that hurdle, the next step is to have a conversation with their billing department. If they are currently invoicing other customers electronically, they will probably readily agree to bill you in the same manner. You might want to alert purchasing to your strategy. They may have some suggestions or may even offer to make the call for you.

The problem arises if they are not currently e-invoicing customers. In this case you may be able to convince them to either e-mail you a pdf of the invoice or fax the invoice to your accounts payable department fax.

There is a second issue you'll need to address honestly. Are you paying the vendor late because of problems on your end? Are those problems in accounts payable or in another department? Unfortunately, if this is the case you should be prepared for some potential push back from the vendor.

Why should they adjust their processes because your organization isn't doing as good a job as it should? Still, if they want to be paid on a timely basis, many will be willing to help out and will work to get you the invoice as quickly as possible. So, don't cross these vendors off your list of prospects to contact.

The Discrepant Invoice Producers

Everyone's got them: suppliers whose invoices are loaded with errors. And, rarely are those errors in your favor. What's worse is these seem to be the guys who are first on the phone to complain when they don't get paid on time. The important factor with these invoices is to get them as quickly as possible so you can begin working on fixing those errors.

Before you go down the e-invoicing route, you might want to make sure that the purchase orders your organization is providing is not causing part of the problem. Talk with purchasing to make sure they are completely filling out their POs. The purchasing executive associated with that account might have some insights on why so many problems are occurring.

Once you are sure the problem is not on your end, contact the vendor to inquire about e-invoicing. If you have the ability to use one of the nifty models now available with online dispute resolution, jump on it. It is probably the answer to this ongoing nightmare.

Assuming you don't, follow the steps above contacting the vendor and if nothing else getting them to email or fax the invoice. The sooner you get their information, the sooner you can identify the problems and work to fix them.

The Early Pay Discount Invoices

These present a real opportunity for accounts payable to make a bottom line difference to the organization. Vendors offering early pay discounts are few and far between so when you do find one, you want to make sure not to lose it. In fact, some organizations track early payment discounts lost each year. It is not a good thing for accounts payable for this to be a large number. It is especially distressing if it is a large amount and the real cause is not with accounts payable but elsewhere because accounts payable is the one who ends up with the black eye on this issue.

The first thing you need to do is figure out why the invoices are getting to accounts payable late. If you don't have all invoices sent to accounts payable first, at least have the early pay discount vendors send their invoices to accounts payable first. Save the envelopes to track where the problem is. Are they being mailed late (which happens occasionally) or are they being delayed with the approver?

If the delay is in your shop, track it and compute the quarterly or annual cost. This is one way to get the attention of approvers who leave invoices on their desks for a week or two. If it is being mailed late contact the vendor. Occasionally the vendor is mailing late because they want to double check their invoices to make sure they are accurate. Other times, their reasons are not so honorable.

Regardless of the real reason, assume the vendor is above board and treat them as such. Again, contact them and ask for e-invoicing and if that is not possible, an email or fax of the invoice. There is no need for finger pointing. The important thing is to get that invoice as quickly as possible to make the early payment cutoff date. A number of suppliers are starting to ask for repayment of that early pay discount from customers who paid after the discount date. Don't let your organization be one of them.

Concluding Thoughts

e-invoicing is the wave of the future. It makes invoice processing in accounts payable run much smoother. Take advantage of it, especially in those problematic situations where you can improve vendor relations at the same time.

Invoice Challenges and How Automation Helps

No matter how automated an organization, virtually all still are plagued by paper invoices. Of course, some have done a fabulous job getting rid of a large number of them, but many others still face the unenviable task of processing mountains of paper. In this article we take a look at eight invoice challenges in a paper world, discuss some solutions as well as offer a brief commentary on if and how automation might help.

Challenge #1: Errors in Manual Data Entry

Tips in a Paper World: Without a doubt, human keying errors create problems for just about any organization entering data manually. Running batch totals is one way to verify that at a minimum, payment amounts have been entered correctly. Some organizations have found that allowing processors to listen to music (with headsets on so others are not disturbed) helps reduce errors also. Finally, a coding standard will help eliminate those errors created when processors are allowed to create their own abbreviations and shortcuts.

How Automation Helps: By eliminating the data entry function, automation eliminates those keying errors made by processors.

Challenge #2: Lack of Consistency when Data Is Entered Manually

Tips in a Paper World: This is one of the easiest problems to create a solution for. A rigid coding standard along with rigid procedures will eliminate the problem. With every processor handling invoices the exactly same way, errors associated with different handling procedures are eliminated. It is not enough to create the ideal process and coding standard, managers need to periodically check to make sure all processors are sticking to the standards and not introducing their own work arounds.

How Automation Helps: Processors handling invoices differently is not a problem in a completely automated invoice processing environment.

Challenge #3: Receipt of Invoices

Tips in a Paper World: In a paper world, invoices are often sent to a variety of places. Some come to accounts payable, some are addressed to no one and are passed from person to person until someone realizes they belong in accounts payable and others are sent to the original purchaser. When invoices don't come directly to accounts payable, additional work is created when vendors call looking for payments on invoices still with approvers. In an ideal paper world (Is that an oxymoron?) invoices are sent to one centralized location for further distribution. This way they can be logged and tracked.

With organizations everywhere looking to cut costs, a number of vendors are refusing to mail invoices. They insist on either emailing or faxing invoices. Therefore, today when we talk about one centralized location, we mean one snail mail address, one email address and one fax number.

How Automation Helps: With invoice automation, copies of invoices can be sent with a few clicks of a mouse. It is relatively easy to receive invoices either centrally and immediately forward to the appropriate parties or to give both parties (accounts payable and purchasing) online visibility to the invoice.

Challenge #4: Invoice Volume

Tips in a Paper World: In a paper world, the sheer number of invoices is a concern. As the number increases, it is sometimes necessary to add staff simply to handle the volume. Many organizations look to p-cards to get many small dollar invoices out of accounts payable. Those organizations dealing with numerous small dollar invoices from the same vendor in a short period of time sometimes decide to pay from weekly or monthly statements instead of individual invoices.

How Automation Helps: When invoice processing is automated, volume is less of a concern. The only exception might be for those using software that charges on a per-invoice basis. In those cases, the organization might want to investigate some of the solutions suggested for the paper world.

Challenge #5: Invoice Routing for Approvals when Approvers Don't Respond

Tips in a Paper World: When invoices are sent out for approval in a paper world, accounts payable does not always know if someone is out on vacation, out unexpectedly or is just not bothering to review the invoices sent. There is no good solution to this problem in a paper world. One partial solution involves developing a list of people known to be negligent in approving invoices and send them regular reminders, perhaps copying their immediate supervisor if they are tardy. This is a bit of work.

How Automation Helps: In an automated world, if approval escalations (sometimes referred to as cascading approvals) are included, the problem goes away. When an invoice is not approved within a preset number of days, the invoice is automatically escalated to the next level for approval. Anecdotal evidence suggests that just including the approval escalation in the process eliminates almost 100% of the tardy approver problem.

Challenge #6: Tracking Invoices

Tips in a Paper World: Whether you are monitoring invoices out for approval or those that have a dispute "issue," keeping track of invoices can be a real headache in a paper world. We suggest tracking and monitoring disputed invoices using an Excel spreadsheet with regular follow-ups and aging to help identify problem spots as well as get invoice issues addressed.

How Automation Helps: When a fully automated invoice processing system is used, an electronic audit trail is created. Thus, at any point in time, anyone with access can view where an invoice is in the process and who touched it, changed it and when. Additionally, special tracking routines can be built into some third party systems during the initial configuration stage.

Challenge #7: Dispute resolution

Tips in a Paper World: In a paper world, dispute resolution boils down to phone calls and emails. It's easy for invoices to fall through the cracks if the matter isn't resolved quickly or it is necessary to get additional documentation. Whether in a paper world or in an electronic environment, dispute resolution typically ends up in accounts payable. This is unfortunate as almost always it is necessary to get purchasing or receiving involved to settle the dispute.

How Automation Helps: When dispute resolution is automated, the problem is posted online. Each party is then responsible for checking to see what items are disputed and then resolving their issue. If they don't fulfill their task by an agreed upon deadline, reminders can be automated as well as escalations.

Challenge #8: Monitoring invoice disputes

Tips in a Paper World: Disputed invoices have a way of disappearing in a paper environment. Unless there is rigorous tracking and follow up, the disputes frequently go unresolved and a second invoice is sent and occasionally paid. If there is no online capability to track invoices with problems, the manager should create an Excel spreadsheet where disputes are tracked and aged. Periodically—ideally weekly—the manager should review the aging and check with the processor responsible for old invoices.

How Automation Helps: If a tracking is built into the invoice processing system, the reports discussed above can be generated automatically and reminders sent. While the manager will still have to get involved from time to time, the amount of management involvement will be diminished. And, of course, they won't have to create the tracking and aging reports. The computer will do it for them.

Paper invoices are here to stay, at least for the time being. Effective managers will deal with the problems they create as part of their overall management function. By recognizing the problems ahead of time, they will be equipped to develop strategies to deal with the headaches created by paper.

Chapter 7: Stopping the Practice of Sending Duplicate Invoices

Submitting duplicate copies of the same invoice has turned into a nightmare for a large number of companies. Over 80% reported this issue in the Nacha/AP Now survey conducted in early 2020. This is up from two-thirds of those responding to an AP Now survey conducted two years earlier. While this has always been a problem, the issue has been magnified due to email. It now costs next to nothing for a vendor to send multiple copies.

Even if the organization is successful in weeding out the duplicate invoices, the time spent identifying the duplicate is non-value add. Valuable human resources are wasted doing so. These folks can and should be doing something else. And of course, a few of those duplicate invoices do get paid and some of those vendors neglect to return the funds.

We acknowledge that a small percentage of those are doing so in the hopes of enticing you to pay twice. But this is not the motivation for the majority.

Your First Plan of Attack

It seems that every improvement brings its own set of problems. This is precisely what happened when more organizations began accepting e-mailed invoices. A growing number of vendors who e-mail invoices also send paper copies through the mail "just to be on the safe side." This of course creates extra work in accounts payable - not exactly the direction most organizations wish to go. We asked readers about the best ways to handle vendors who insist on sending invoices by e-mail and snail mail.

What we found is there is no golden solution – but some of our readers were effectively dealing with the situation. What follows is a look at how they are combatting the problem.

The Basic Approach: Stopping the Duplicates

I personally haven't found a good way to get vendors to NOT send the original by snail mail and emailing a copy also, wrote several managers. Some of my vendors have been nice and not sending the original, but only by calling and begging them not to mail them if they email, points out one of them. Some are nice and some are not.

An Aggressive, but Effective Solution

Reject paper invoices, says a responding supervisor. She notes that one of the companies she worked for in the past wanted to work to achieve a 100% paperless environment, by accepting electronic invoices via EDI and e-mail. The organization had an aggressive notification campaign by sending letters to vendors, including letters in their checks, and also put a message on their remittance advice which covered vendors being paid electronically. They told the vendors that all paper invoices would be rejected and thrown in the trash.

There were some small companies that did not have the capability to send electronic invoices so there was a small percentage of paper still coming into the department but the list of vendors to process paper invoices was small.

We should note that we heard from several e-invoicing software companies who pointed out that their products would solve the problem, weeding out duplicate invoices.

It's not only e-Mailed Invoices

Snail mail vs. email can certainly create issues, responded another manager, snail mail alone can still cause problems. A very large company with multiple well-known brand names always issues two invoice copies for each shipment, he explains. One invoice copy is enclosed with the shipment directly to the retail location (we operate 11 locations in 5 states), the other copy is mailed to our corporate PO Box.

This would be bad enough, except there is another issue. "All would be fine," he explains," except the invoice number shown on the mailed copy includes a series of leading zeros that do not appear on the ship-to copy.

To help our Dynamics GP system reliably warns us of duplicate invoice numbers, our rule is to always add the leading zeros to this vendor's invoice number."

Dealing with the Issue

Given that it appears this is a problem that will be with us for some time, some of our readers have developed procedures to deal with it. They include the following.

1) We always send our Requirement document to the vendors who ask about our electronic/ emailed invoice option. It says, "Accounts Payable would love to partner with you on submitting invoices to us electronically however, please note our requirements for receiving invoices electronically at our invoices@.com mailbox."

- ✓ Only one invoice attachment per email is accepted.

- ✓ Accepted formats are PDF, Word, or Excel.

- ✓ Invoice number should be listed in the subject line to avoid documents combining into one.

- ✓ All invoices must contain a PO Number or Accounting Unit number and Full Name of person ordering product/service.

- ✓ No password protection or embedded links to obtain document can be sent.

- ✓ Only original invoices. No statements, past due or correspondence should be sent to this mailbox. Statements, correspondence, etc. should be sent to accountspayable@.com.

- ✓ Paper copies of invoices should not be mailed. This will become your invoice for payment.

2) To tackle duplicate invoicing in our organization, our software in Accounts Payable catches duplicate invoices automatically. But; not everyone enters them the same way. If, for instance there are dashes within an invoice number, and it gets paid with the "dash" and another duplicate invoice gets mailed, faxed or emailed and it gets entered again this time without the dash, it won't catch. The solution was to bring this up in our on-going training sessions to enter invoice numbers exactly the way they

appear on the invoice, including the dashes, letters before the number, example: INV12345. We ask our users to be consistent when entering invoice numbers and to follow the AP guidelines we have in place. So far, we have been successful in duplicating.

On a Regular Basis

This problem will not go away. Even if you think you have it under control, some vendors will revert to their old bad habits and new ones will discover that email costs next to nothing and will start. Here are some steps you can use to minimize this issue:

Step 1: Identify the culprits and ask them to stop. This step will have to be repeated periodically.

Step 2: Make sure none of your employees are sabotaging your efforts by asking suppliers to send them a copy also – and then they forward it to accounts payable for payment.

Step 3: Pay on time. Vendors are within their rights to submit a second copy of the invoice, if you haven't paid them within the agreed upon payment terms.

Step 4: Create an automated notification to your vendors telling them you have their invoice. If you can indicate an approximate payment date, do so. It will help to reduce those annoying calls asking when payment will be made.

Step 5: Start using an invoice automation process, selecting a service provider that is capable of sending the automated notice to the vendor indicated in Step 4. Invoice automation systems that have an online payment status function that the vendor can use to check payment dates

While it is probably not realistic to think you can completely eliminate this problem, you can certainly make a big dent in it.

Concluding Thoughts

This issue will be with us for some time to come. The importance of best practices and duplicate payment checking continue. They are critical for identifying those duplicate invoices before they get paid. As time goes on and increasing numbers of invoices are sent electronically, perhaps this problem will diminish. But, for the present, stringent coding standards and standardized practices are critical for catching those problematic second invoices.

Other Tactics to Help Eliminate Duplicate Invoices

While it may be next to impossible to completely eliminate duplicate payments, it's certainly possible to get the number down to a miniscule figure. By following all the practices enumerated below you will be able to accomplish that goal. Why am I so sure? Because I've seen organizations that rigidly adhere to the guidelines all but eliminate them. There can be no exceptions to these steps—because exceptions open the door for duplicates.

- Use detailed coding standards. This is a three-pronged approach. There needs to be one policy for invoice data entry. This should be coordinated with the naming convention used when setting up vendors in the master vendor file. Issues like how initials should be handled (IBM or I.B.M. etc) should be spelled out and all processors required to use the agreed upon standard. Finally, develop a standard for invoice number data entry. This is especially important if your system limits the number of data fields for the invoice number.

- Develop a standard for creating an invoice number for invoices without invoice numbers. This standard should create a unique invoice number for each invoice that arrives without a number. The same number should result from your routine regardless of who creates the number and when. This is crucial. Some experts estimate that as many as 40% of all invoices do not have invoice numbers. Note: Some organizations refuse to accept invoices without invoice numbers and return them to the vendor asking for a unique invoice number.

- Make all payments within the agreed upon timeframe. Stretching payments, whether from need or to improve cash flow, will result in a second invoice being sent. How good your processes are will determine how many of those second invoices make it through and get paid. Don't assume your processes are so iron tight that this won't occur. A few crafty vendors will actually change the invoice number on the second invoice.

- Have all invoices sent to accounts payable first. This will ensure the invoices are all identified and aren't lost in the mail somewhere. A side benefit is that this makes earning early payment discounts easier. There is a rapidly growing movement to deliver invoices by e-mail and fax. These e-mail addresses and fax numbers should be sent to accounts payable.

- Pay extra attention to large-dollar invoices. When it comes to duplicate payments, all invoices are definitely not created equal. Develop some extra checking routines around large invoices to be completely certain a duplicate payment is not being made. The definition of large will vary from organization to organization.

- Pay extra attention to past due invoices. There is a chance they have already been paid, perhaps using an alternate payment vehicle such as a wire transfer or p-card. Develop routines to check that payment hasn't been made whenever an invoice that is really past due is presented for payment.

- Vendors who can be paid with multiple payment vehicles also deserve extra attention. Ideally, each vendor should be paid in only one way, i.e. only checks, only p-cards etc. However, in real life, this doesn't always work. Develop special checking routines for the few vendors that do not adhere to the one payment methodology.

- Train those making payments outside accounts payable to use the same rigid standards as used inside the department. This especially means that receivers and POs must be extinguished when a wire transfer or ACH payment is made. The lack of this conformity is one of the leading reasons duplicate payments are shooting up again.

- Employ really good master vendor file practices. This means using the coding standard discussed above as well as regularly cleansing the master vendor file. Ideally, a report should be run of all changes made to the master vendor file each week. This report should be delivered to a senior executive who reviews it. The real purpose of this report is to prevent employees from playing games with the file for fraudulent purposes. However, it also helps keep the master vendor file in check.

- If your volume of transactions is large enough, consider establishing an internal audit position that reviews for duplicate payments before a third-party audit firm is brought in. This allows you to find the low-hanging fruit yourself and only pay the duplicate payment audit firm for those difficult-to-find items.

- Hire a third-party auditor, ideally working on a contingency basis, to find any outstanding duplicates. If you are doing most of what is suggested in this piece, it is likely the recoveries will be low. If, however, you only think you are employing these tactics and your employees are doing something else, the recoveries will be higher. Take advantage of the Executive Report provided by the firm at the end of the engagement. This should provide you with a list of weaknesses in your processes that allow duplicates to slip through.

- Eliminate poor practices that facilitate duplicate payments. Many of these will be listed in the report provided by the third-party auditor. Probably the most important steps to implement in your war against duplicate payments are the strict coding standards and the timely payment practices. And don't assume because you told your processors to do something six months ago that all are doing it today. Periodically check. You may be shocked at what you discover.

- As you can see, the recommended steps are within the reach of virtually every organization. Like a new diet or exercise program it's just a matter of deciding to do it, in this case getting management buy-in, training the staff, and then periodically checking to make sure everyone is continuing to do as instructed. Okay, maybe it isn't simple but it is certainly within the grasp of everyone reading this article.

Mystery Invoices

Do you receive too many invoices with neither a PO number on them nor the name of the person who ordered the goods? Does your staff waste its time trying to figure out if the invoice is legitimate and who ordered the items in question? This is a colossal waste of time. What's more, sometimes you spend so much time trying to figure out who should approve the invoice for payment, the invoice becomes past due. Then the vendor sends a second invoice.

There is a better way to address this matter and it doesn't waste your staff's time. Write a polite letter informing the supplier of your requirement that every invoice have either a PO number or a requistioner's name. Send the invoice with the letter back every time you receive such an invoice.

Make sure all your purchasers are aware of this policy as they can save suppliers time by informing them of this requirement. Your letter can serve a dual purpose if you include an address where the invoice should be returned. This will put a dent in the other problem that some organizations have with invoices – the fact that they are sent all over the organization, sometimes taking weeks to get to accounts payable.

One organization that took this approach reports that it completely eliminated this problem. While the staff thought the vendors might complain, at the end of the day, all they wanted to do was get paid. So, they were more than happy to comply.

Finally, if your organization seems to have numerous invoices that fall outside your guidelines, consider sending a letter to all vendors telling them:

- Where they should send the invoice (your correct bill-to address).
- The fact that it must contain a PO or purchaser's name.
- Your terms (this prevents unrealistic expectations on the part of the vendor).

Dirty Invoice Trick Some Vendors Play

There are some consultants who are advising their clients to improve cash flow by sending a second invoice the day the payment is due. Clearly that does not give them adequate time to apply cash for payments made on the due date. That's bad enough. But other consultants advise their clients to send a second copy of the invoice five days before the due date.

Clearly this makes it more imperative than ever to carefully vet for duplicate copies of invoices. Should you discover a supplier is doing this, bring the matter to the attention of the purchasing manager and ask him/her to discuss it with the supplier.

Chapter 8: Crisis Payment Issues: Duplicate Payments and Returned Checks

Duplicate payments will become a huge issue for some organizations as they struggle through the crisis. Even if you don't normally have a payment audit done, it is something you might want to consider three to six months after we return to "normal" – whatever that may turn out to be. For more information on the issue of audits, please see Chapter 19. Now, before we address duplicate payments and what you can do to address that headache, let's look at the newest issue facing many companies.

The New Nuisance for AP: Some organizations that are closed are not receiving mail. The post office is returning mail, including any checks you may have sent them for payment.

Handling the Problem: These will have to be reconciled upon the return to the office and possibly reissued. But rather than reissue, take this opportunity to contact the vendor and ask if they will accept electronic payments. Before reissuing the payment, double check to make sure you have not already paid them.

One Other Caveat: If a vendor calls looking for a past-due payment and your records show you issued a check more than a day or two ago, inquire if they are having mail delivered. Also, if you decide to pay them electronically, make sure you get the check back before authorizing the electronic payment. And when you do, follow your standard procedures for voiding a payment, including removing it from the Positive Pay file.

Duplicate Payment Avoidance

The very best protection against duplicate payments is to make sure they don't happen in the first place. Now, if you're thinking "Duh – we know that" realize that not making them in the first place is not as easy as it sounds. What's more, some executives firmly believe their organization never makes a duplicate payment and alas, they are rarely correct. It's like the people who say they never make a mistake. Best practices that help prevent duplicate payments in the first place include:

- Use of best practices and strong internal controls around the master vendor file

- Timely payment of the original invoice

- Use of rigid coding standards for data entry when processing invoices

- Reducing or eliminating all Rush checks

- Regularly cleansing the master vendor file of inactive and duplicate vendors

- Each time a duplicate payment is identified, review the paperwork to see if you can identify the root cause. Once that cause has been identified, work to eliminate the problem.

Duplicate payments will happen, regardless of how tight the controls are. Accounts payable is often concerned that they will be unfairly blamed for any duplicate payments. Occasionally that happens. More often, it provides accounts payable with the ammunition needed to get the changes they want implemented. Too often, accounts payable knows that processes should be changed or improved but it cannot get the resources or support needed to implement those changes.

There is another untold tale related to duplicate payment audit firms. Some of them report that they go back to the same companies year after year, finding the same type of duplicate payments over and over again. It's not that the audit firm hasn't given recommendations for change – the company has just not implemented them.

Insist that the duplicate payment audit firm not only recover funds, but also identify procedural weak spots in your organization. The firms should also make recommendations as to what the company can do to tighten its policies and procedures. The recommendations from the audit firm are often the turning point that gets management moving.

The Duplicate-Payments Sad Facts

In an AP Now survey of several hundred AP professionals we asked participants if within the last three years they had ever had a supplier return a check indicating it was a duplicate. Just under 95% indicated they had. To be exact, 94.92% said they'd had a check returned by an honest vendor. Now, as most reading this are ever-so-painfully aware, few vendors will actually return the duplicate payment. Most deposit it and hope you never figure it out.

Okay, maybe I'm a bit cynical. Maybe their processes don't allow for the easy identification of the duplicate. Whatever the case, the 95% figure combined with the fact that most duplicates aren't returned, leads to my thesis that virtually every organization makes duplicate payments. We also asked to what department these checks were returned. The majority (83.93%) thankfully, are returned to accounts payable. The remaining checks are returned to:

- The general mailing address

- The controller

- The CFO

- Transportation

- Accounts receivable

The list is in descending order, with the largest number going to the general mailing address, then the controller etc.

And, as you might imagine, the reaction when the check ends up anyplace but accounts payable is rarely positive. Some organizations try to figure out how it happened so they can prevent it in the future. That's a really good idea. Others demand to know how it could have happened in the first place. This accusatory approach is not so great. In fact, one participant describes the response to it as "one of massive confusion."

And, finally, a few respondents indicated that no one in their organization bats an eye when a check is returned by a vendor indicating it is a duplicate. Why aren't they the least bit surprised? Because, as one wrote, "Our invoice distributions are such a mess, it's not unexpected that some invoices get paid twice."

Are Things Getting Better?

We wondered if the increased awareness of the problem has made organizations more careful. Now, keep in mind something about duplicate payments. Like fraud, people can only report on the duplicates that they know about. If duplicate payments have been made but not identified, the assumption is they don't exist. And there is sometimes a reticence to admit mistakes although given the 95% figure at the beginning of the article, this discretion appears to have all but disappeared.

We asked respondents if they thought the number of duplicate payments at their organization had decreased as compared with three years ago. Slightly more than half (50.85%) said they thought the number had declined. Don't assume that the other half reported making a larger number of duplicate payments; that is not the case. Over one third (37.29%) indicated that they simply did not know whether the number of duplicates had increased at their organization. Only about 12% thought they had increased.

The Year-End Problem

When checking for duplicates, many systems will go back anywhere from 30 to 90 days to see if the payment was made. However, for a variety of reasons, this checking often does not go from year to year. Hence, a payment processed in February will not be checked against payments made in December of the prior year.

Some duplicate-payment auditors report that a good portion of their recoveries come from payments made in two different years. Make sure your duplicate payment checking routines go over year end.

Prevention: Controls, Training, and Standards

While many keep the number of their duplicates down to a small number, even one is too many. Constant vigilance is required to keep the number of duplicates to a real minimum. We asked survey participants about the success so many clearly have had in reducing these payments. We present the best of their techniques in the accompanying table.

Three themes came through in their responses. Tight controls surrounding invoice processing helps reduce duplicate payments as does continued staff training and standards. The standards should be set for:

- Master vendor file

- Invoice coding

- Creating an invoice number for invoices without an invoice number

- Staff processing

- Invoice handling

Tactics Company Use to Reduce Duplicate Payments

1) Tighter controls.

2) More controls on purchase order (PO) matching process.

3) More controls and reporting on adjustments to orders (especially after dispatching initial order).

4) More controls on invoice number entry schema.

5) Improved/increased training of staff to improve consistency in combination with updated processes that occasionally catch more duplicates.

6) Being more alert and diligent in looking out for chances for duplicate payments.

7) An internal system of creating an appropriate invoice number reference when an invoice number is not used by a vendor.

8) Duplicate payment audits pointing out deficiencies.

9) Policies for invoice numbering and vendor set up.

10) Tighter surveillance. System (computer) controls enhanced.

11) More training of personnel.

12) Staffing consistency and improved educational practices.

13) Use of a third-party audit company to find the problem areas and give solutions.

14) Data entry standardization.

15) Changing the way the address book is set up.

16) Eliminate duplicate vendors account records.

17) Standardized invoice numbering.

18) Weekly audits and report on possible duplicates.

19) A change in the computer to not check due dates when comparing invoice numbers for duplication.

20) Tighter management of vendor maintenance access and voucher approval process.

21) Tight invoice numbering guidelines, which addresses how to number an invoice when the vendor has no number.

22) Being more aware of the invoice numbers.

23) Better scrutiny of payments for invoices that do not come in with assigned invoice numbers.

24) Duplicate payment software.

25) Tighter controls on processing copies of invoices.

26) Requiring purchase orders for most payments.

27) AP coordinator approval of all payments from invoice copies after researched in system, and a systems report (invoice numbers allocated twice) is run once or twice a month.

28) Entering invoice numbers exactly as they appear on the invoice.

29) Entering date spans for telephone, utility, etc. bills as the invoice number.

30) Checking vendor records for invoices with no date span or invoice number.

31) Reinforcing controls and standards in coding invoices.

Stop Duplicate Payments in Their Tracks: A 13-Step Precautionary Plan of Attack.

Duplicate payments insidiously eat away at any organization's bottom line. They are the dirty little secret in corporate accounting and financial circles. Even those organizations that piously claim they never make a duplicate payment have them. There are just too many ways these payments can get made. Like the person who says they never make a mistake, this claim does not stand up under the harsh light of day.

The realistic goal of any accounts payable organization when it comes to duplicate payments should be threefold:

1)   Don't make any duplicate payments;

2)   Since we know that number one is unlikely, the secondary fallback position should be to identify duplicates and erroneous payments before they go out the door; and

3)   Should the secondary goal fail, as it occasionally will, identify the dupes after the fact and reclaim those funds.

The Action Plan

Once you've taken the first step of recognizing that there is a problem you are ready to implement a comprehensive action plan to decimate it. What follows are a dozen steps you can take to accomplish this goal.

1)   Use coding standards for both your master vendor file and invoice data entry to minimize the chance of an invoice slipping through a second time.

2)   Eliminate duplicate vendors from your master vendor file. Once you've identified a duplicate vendor, make sure the data gets merged in with the file that will remain. You do not want to lose any supplier payment history.

3)   Do everything possible to eliminate the need for the supplier to send a second invoice. This includes paying at or near term and keeping the vendor informed of any change to your standard terms.

4)   Check records for any payment over $50,000 before releasing the check. The $50,000 number is not set in stone and should be adjusted to a level appropriate for each organization.

5)   Before releasing checks, run a list of the dollar amounts of all checks issued in the prior 90 days and check for any duplicate amounts. If multiple invoices are paid with one check this approach is less likely to spot duplicates.

6)   Keep track of every invoice that enters accounts payable, including disputed invoices. Never just send an invoice back to purchasing for reconciliation with a supplier without entering it in a log so you can answer any inquiries about it. This helps prevent the vendor from sending a second invoice.

7) Once you've located duplicate payments, keep track of the root causes. Periodically, perhaps quarterly, analyze all your potential duplicates and try to eliminate the problem areas generating the most duplicates.

8) Should your organization install a new accounting system, or even go through a system upgrade, take special care in searching for potential duplicates. Should an invoice show up for payment dated prior to the system switchover, make sure to check the old system to see if the payment was made.

9) Occasionally vendors will change the invoice number on second copies of invoices. This may be something as simple as adding a letter at the end of the invoice number or something more insidious. Whether this is done for a less than honest reason is irrelevant. It will wreak havoc with your duplicate payment tracking processes that depend on the invoice number as most do. Keep a list of such vendors and double check all their invoices when processing for payment.

10) Periodically cleanse your vendor file. Ideally this should be done quarterly but most organizations manage to get it done annually. Any vendor with no activity for the prior 12 months should be deactivated. Do not delete the vendor or you will lose the payment history. This can be important should the supplier claim non-payment.

11) Never pay from a statement unless an arrangement has been made with a supplier to only pay from statements. You might do this with vendors who submit many small-dollar invoices throughout the month. If you employ such a practice it should be an all-or-nothing affair. Also, your system should be flagged to prevent the processing of invoices from this vendor.

12) At least once a year request statements from all vendors. The letter should categorically state that you want it to include all activity including open credits. A good portion of credits are duplicate payments. You can either request that a check be issued for those credits (my preference as it keeps a clean audit trail) or take those credits against future invoices. Also use these statements to identify older invoices that have not made their way into accounts payable. Do not pay from the statement.

13) Periodically, say once a year, hire a duplicate payment audit firm to search for duplicates that managed to slip through your almost-iron-clad system.

Track the Data

Once you've implemented whichever of the action steps outlined above you found appropriate for your organization, you might want to keep track of the number of duplicate payments found in that thirteenth step. After several years, compare the amount the audit firms were finding before you stepped up your duplicate payment prevention program with afterwards. If the results are less favorable, it is time to reconnoiter and figure out what is going wrong. Once you've done that you can tighten the controls around the process that is letting money slip away.

However, in all likelihood, this will not be the case. Assuming the results are favorable for your group, report this in a detailed memo to management. What a great way to highlight the contributions your group is making to the organization's profitability!

Use Technology to Minimize Duplicate Payments.

Most organizations have made great strides in eradicating duplicate payments. They insist on stringent coding standards, regularly cleanse their master vendor file and have standardized their invoice handling processes. While these actions certainly will make a big dent in the duplicate payment issue, they won't completely eliminate the problem. The following three steps, which rely heavily on technology, will help identify those invoices that still slip through a second time, despite the best practices you've already integrated into your process.

Step 1. Rely on the invoice number limitation that prevents the entering of a duplicate invoice number in your ERP system, if it has that capability. For this tool to do full duty, it is critical that your invoice processors understand the importance of entering the invoice number correctly and not monkeying around with it, if it shows as a duplicate. Too often, processors simply modify the invoice number slightly to force an invoice through. In reality, the fact that the ERP system is signaling it as a duplicate should be a red flag that it is likely a duplicate invoice.

Step 2. Use duplicate payment checking routines inherent in your ERP system before payments are released. Too often this functionality is turned off or was never turned on, when the system was first installed. This is unfortunate because the organization has paid for functionality that is not being used and could save thousands or millions of dollars.

Step 3. Create simple Excel routines to check for duplicate payments before the payments are released. These can be created using the conditional formatting function and are relatively easy to run. This checking is especially important when running checks at the beginning of a new fiscal year or when there has been a system upgrade or a migration to a new system. All these events are likely to trigger an increase in potential duplicate payments. So, this extra checking is well worth the time involved.

Concluding Thoughts

Clearly, you can run more sophisticated analysis, using data mining and analytics, if your staff has both the capability and time. While your good practices throughout the procure-to-pay process combined with the routines suggested above will certainly help identify duplicate payments before the payments leaves your door, a few will still slip though. That's where statement audits can help. Conduct these audits on a very regular basis. They are the best way to ensure you have collected all your vendor credits, some of which may have been created by duplicate payments. If you don't have the time or resources necessary to handle complete statement audits of all your vendors, have a third-party firm conduct one for you.

How to Use Excel's Conditional Formatting to Find Duplicates

The conditional formatting feature in Excel is an extremely useful feature for those analyzing or simply using accounts payable data. You can find the conditional formatting tab on the main home portion of your ribbon. It is approximately at the midpoint. Let's take a look at four simple applications that will help any accounts payable team improve their operations. This process can be used when looking for duplicate payments, duplicate invoices or duplicate entries in the master vendor file.

- ✓ Begin by putting all the information in an excel spreadsheet.

- ✓ Highlight the column you want to search for duplicate values. Note: If you don't limit this to one or two columns but let the entire worksheet be searched, it will take a long time and will report on duplicates you don't care about. For example, if you had addresses in the file, it might report duplicate entries in the state column.

- ✓ Hit the conditional formatting tab. Several options will show up.

- ✓ Select the find duplicate values tab. It is the last option in most versions of Excel.

- ✓ You will then be given the option of selecting how you want the duplicate data to be shown – in red, green etc.

Once you have the data highlighted, you'll need to sort it to easily identify the duplicates. In most cases, additional research will be needed to ensure the potential duplicates are true. You can expect some false positives. Often recurring payment for items such as rent will appear to be duplicates at first glance. But, upon further investigation, they will get checked off your list.

Losing the Duplicate Payments War? These Five Practices May Be to Blame!

Duplicate payments continue to be a top issue for many of our readers. While many have plugged some of the obvious holes, AP Now has identified five practices that are often overlooked in the battle. Pinpointing these issues and strengthening the internal controls around them, will better position readers to win the duplicate-payment war. Let's take a look at the practices.

1. Invoices paid by check request forms in case of emergency can inadvertently create a situation where the duplicate payment can slip through. Since the three-way match is often not utilized when processing check requests, the purchase order and receiver often remain open. Then when the original invoice finally shows up in accounts payable for payment it is processed through the standard payment process and paid a second time. What's even worse is these check request payments are sometimes made without backup so tying them to a particular invoice is difficult if not impossible.

2. The data entry practice for entering invoice numbers occasionally fosters duplicate payments. Most organizations know they should incorporate invoice coding standards and have done so. This greatly decreases the chance of a duplicate payment. However, what some don't crack down on are the nifty ways processors sometimes have for working around the controls. Virtually all processors know that by simply adding a space or a period or another digit or letter to an invoice number they can force the invoice through their system. Successful managers make their staff understand how serious it is to take that step and a few even make it an offense to be entered in their personnel file.

3. Payments made outside AP by employees not fully schooled in strict accounts payable routines can cause duplicates. With the move to ACH and p-cards, a decent number of organizations are allowing payments to be made by employees outside the accounts payable organization. On the face of it, there is nothing wrong with this. However, if these employees are not trained using the strict coding standards employed in accounts payable, or they do not correctly close out the purchase order and/or the receiving document, the chance for a duplicate payment looms. Additionally, although not related to payments, not properly closing these related documents could lead to inaccurate financial statements and additional work as someone has to review open receivers.

4. Lack of a single payment mechanism to pay each vendor often results in payment being made by both p-card and invoice. While it is a theoretical best practice that each vendor be paid using only one payment vehicle, Accounts Payable Now & Tomorrow understands that in practice this is not always feasible. More than a few p-card vendors claim they cannot suppress the printing of the invoice and in theory most are marked either with a zero balance due or that the invoice has been paid by p-card. In any case where a dual payment mechanism is possible, controls need to be incorporated to ensure an item isn't paid for twice. Third-party auditors report that much of their recoveries come from this one issue.

5. Not sorting out duplicate copies of invoices. In the past it was relatively easy to discern a faxed copy of an invoice or a second invoice. Today, with the advances in printing and e-mail, it is no longer so simple and it's often impossible to tell which is the original and which is the copy. Suppliers regularly send pdfs of invoices— and who can spot if it's the first time the invoice was received or a later copy? While it's still a good idea to refuse to pay from copies or faxes, that approach won't provide you with the same protection it did just a few short years ago.

While it's probably not possible to completely eliminate duplicate payments, by identifying the issues that can lead to them and taking appropriate preventative steps, you can greatly reduce their number—and with minimal effort.

Real-Life Duplicate Payments at Best Practice Organizations

"Duplicate payments? Oh no, not in my shop!" Everyone likes to think that and some of us actually say it but reality, alas, tells a different story. What follows is a look at five actual duplicate payments and the weaknesses in the organizations' processes that allowed them to slip through. We also offer solutions that, had they been in place, might very well have prevented the duplicate. It should be noted that the organizations where these duplicates occurred were not generally known for sloppy processes yet through tiny cracks in their controls came giant duplicate payments. Let's take a look at what happened.

Case #1: Duplicate Payment Amount: $3.6 million

Cause: Payments made using two different payment vehicles, in this case a paper check and a wire transfer.

Solution: * Use the same strong payment controls around wire transfers (and ACH) as used with paper checks.

    * If payments are made outside AP, insist staff making payments adhere to the same strict procedures used within accounts payable.

    * Mandate that POs and receivers be extinguished when a payment is made regardless of the payment vehicle.

Case # 2: Duplicate Payment Amount: $300,000 (cumulative)

Cause: Consultant called each month and screamed and hollered at the processor.

Solution: * View loud abrasive vendors with skepticism, especially at organizations with good payment practices. This is one of the oldest scams in the book.

    * Require backup for every rush check and then make sure the affiliated PO is extinguished.

    * Incorporate the same stringent practices around check requests as you do around invoices.

Case #3: Duplicate Payment Amount: $76,000

Cause: The check was returned to the requisitioner who did not immediately give it to the vendor. A new check was issued and a stop payment never issued on the original check—which the requisitioner eventually found and mailed. Both checks were cashed.

Solution: * Never return checks to requisitioners. Insist on a company policy of only mailing checks.

   * If corporate culture is such that a not returning checks to requisitioners is not possible, develop a form that must be signed by a senior executive. The form should include a statement of why the check must be returned. Keep in mind that returning checks could be considered a sign of weak controls in a S-Ox audit.

Case #4: Duplicate Payment Amount: $1.1 million (cumulative)

Cause: Checks returned to requisitioner—who was stealing them!

Solution: * Never return checks to requisitioners.

   * When check request forms are used, inspect the backup closely.

   * When there are variances on the budget vs. actual reports, investigate the causes aggressively.

Case #5: Duplicate Payment Amount: $53,000

Cause: Insufficient backup for a check request. When the original invoice showed up, it was paid since the affiliated PO was still open.

Solution: * Eliminate the use of check request forms for invoice payments. Demand the invoice.

   * If your process still requires a check request form for rush payments, attach the invoice and go through the normal three-way match.

   * Centralize the receipt of all invoices in accounts payable reducing the odds that the invoice will be lost in the system.

Wrap Up

As you can see from these cases, while the amounts of money involved were significant, there was no one egregious error that allowed the duplicates to get through. By adhering to generally accepted accounts payable best practices, most of these duplicates could have been avoided.

Chapter 9. A More Efficient and Cost-Effective Payment Process

The COVID-19 crisis spotlighted, for many, the weaknesses in a payment process that relies heavily on paper checks. It created serious problems for those who often times had to send one or two people into the office in order to get payments made.

Tactics to A More Efficient and Cost-Effective Payment Process

It's relentless; the crusade to drive efficiency through every single process in the organization. When it comes to accounts payable most of the focus, with good reason, is on invoice processing. Lots of progress has been made in that regard. But processing invoices is only half the battle. Making the payment once the invoice has been approved and verified is another huge block of work, comprised of a number of steps. The possibility of improved efficiency in that regard should not be overlooked.

Cost cutting can be achieved in one of two ways:

    A. You can make the process more efficient (reduce or eliminate manual processes that add little or no value) and/or

    B. You can reduce costs

Let's take a look at ten tactics any organization can use to make their payment process either more efficient, more cost effective or both.

Efficiency Savings

When your process is more efficient, inherently, it saves the organization money. Here are a few strategies you can use to achieve that goal.

Tactic #1: Convert as many paper check payments to ACH as possible. Paper checks cost more than many people realize. It's not only the expense of the paper check, the envelope and the postage, but also the people costs associated with intensive manual processes. These expenses relate not only to the issuance of the checks but also the reconciliation and follow up on uncashed checks.

Tactic #2: Consider outsourcing check printing to your bank. At the end of the day, printing checks is not a core competency of any entity, except perhaps the banks. There is no reason to waste valuable, and expensive, human resources on it. Once you have the check issuance process down tight, turn the last steps over to the pros.

Tactic #3: If printing checks, do not take them to the mail room until right before the checks go to the post office. Taking checks to the mail room earlier increases the risk of check fraud since, in most organizations, there are numerous parties walking in and out of a mailroom all day.

Tactic #4: Move as many small dollar purchases to payment with p-cards instead of paper checks. Depending on how efficient your processes are, the cost to process an invoice can run anywhere from $5 to $50. Why are you spending this on invoices of low value? A better practice is to push all purchases below $100 or $500 to a card, assuming the seller accepts cards.

Tactic #5: If you are putting manual signatures on certain checks, consider raising the limit. Some organizations still insist on getting one or more manual signatures on paper checks over a certain dollar level. While this extra round of scrutiny (signers are supposed to review the backup before signing—otherwise the effort is wasted) may be warranted with extremely large payments, that is often not the case. If applicable, analyze the number of times signers actually find errors. Then review your review limits with an eye towards raising them—unless of course, your signers are finding errors.

Cost Cutting/Saving Measures

Taking a close look at the way you make payments, with an eye towards what each approach costs, you will find ways to cut costs without impacting the service provided regarding making payments.

Tactic #6: Replace wires with ACH, wherever possible. Wires are expensive and ACH is not. It's that simple. Keep in mind that there is no dollar limit on ACH transactions, although if you need same day settlement, the limit is currently $25,000 going to $100,000 on March 20,2020.

Tactic #7: Replace Rush wires with Same Day ACH, if under $25,009 ($100,000 after March 20, 2020. The newest option offered by banks for same day settlement removed the objection some had to ACH, if settlement is required on the same day.

Tactic #8: Replace checks delivered by expensive overnight delivery services with ACH. Overnight delivery service can be quite expensive, much more than ACH, even Same Day ACH. With either variety of ACH, the money is put directly into the vendor's bank account, saving them the trouble of having to take the check to the bank. The funds are also available immediately, unlike a check, which may have a short clearing period (of one or more days) before the bank allows use of the funds.

Tactic #9: Choose the most appropriate payment vehicle factoring in cost. So, while a purchase card might be appropriate for smaller payments, some vendors will balk at the suggestion that they take it for larger items. ACH is generally the preferred method of payment, if the vendor will accept it. The cost is low and there is no chance of it getting lost in the mail or bouncing. Checks, despite all their drawbacks, remain a popular choice in the United States while wires are frequently used for large international payments.

Tactic #10: If you have both a travel card and a p-card program, and are only getting a rebate on the p-card program, consider combining the two for a larger rebate. Also, if you have a fuel card program, consider adding that in to the mix, as well.

Concluding Thoughts

Not enough professionals give serious thought to reengineering their payment process with an eye towards making it more efficient and cost effective. Many simply take it for granted. They may shop around for the credit card program that offers the best rates and the highest rebate, but few steps back and look at what they are actually paying to make payments. Sometimes, as discussed above, there is another approach that costs less but yields the same result.

Now, to be fair, sometimes the payment process is tied to the banking arrangement and the company agreed to issue checks through a particular bank as part of its overall banking and financing needs. But that is not frequent.

By reviewing your current process, you may be able to take advantage of some of the tactics discussed in this piece and use them to create an equally effective but more efficient payment process for your organization.

Current Payment Practices

Mid-2019, long before anyone had ever heard of the coronavirus, AP Now surveyed its members to see where they stood on various issues, including payments. The data below reveals how companies in the US were making their B2B payments.

Checks

The good news is, there is progress concerning the reduction of checks—the payment method associated with the highest process costs. Per the graph below, check usage has dropped notably since 2016 and the percentage using checks for at least half of their B2B payments is under 50%.

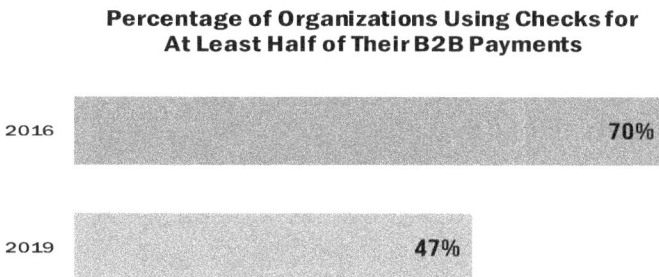

Percentage of Organizations Using Checks for At Least Half of Their B2B Payments

Year	Percentage
2016	70%
2019	47%

Figure 9-1 Organizations Using Checks for B2B Payments

ACH

The results on ACH usage offer more good news. While the percentage of ACH-using organizations has remained in the mid-80% range since 2016, ACH has taken a larger role in their payment strategies. Supporting the reduction of checks, more than 40% of ACH-using organizations rely on ACH for at least half of their B2B payments, as shown below.

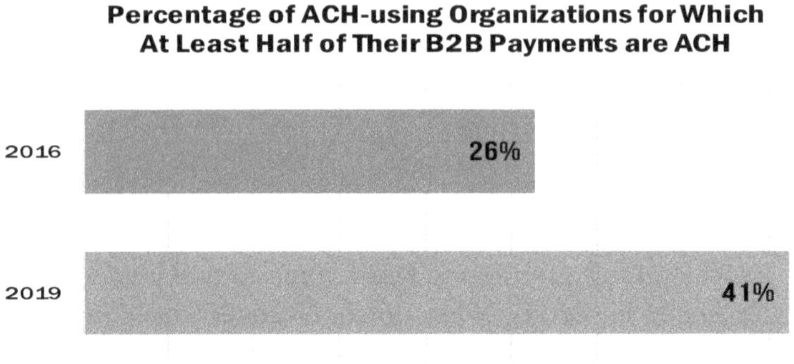

Percentage of ACH-using Organizations for Which At Least Half of Their B2B Payments are ACH

2016	26%
2019	41%

Figure 9-2 Organizations Using ACH for B2B Payments

Cards

Survey results concerning commercial/company cards are not as positive as the ACH results. While the percentage of organizations indicating they have some type of card program is more than 80% card use among them is not as strong as it could be. The breakdown is shown in the graph on the following page

While there is the expectation that ACH programs will grow, given the difficulty some organizations had in issuing checks, only time will tell if that prediction comes true.

Percentage of B2B Payments Comprised by Cards
(among card users only)

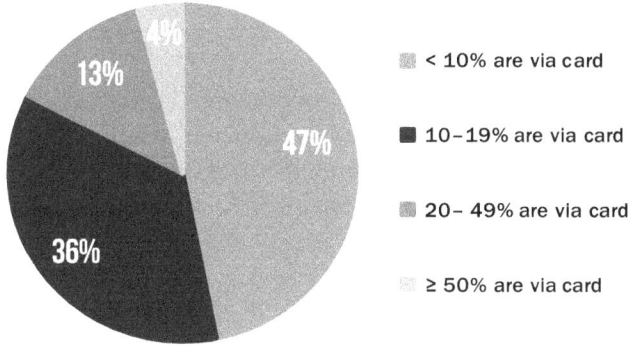

- < 10% are via card
- 10–19% are via card
- 20– 49% are via card
- ≥ 50% are via card

Figure 9-3 Organizations Using Cards for B2B Payments

Ten Tactics to A More Efficient and Cost-Effective Payment Process

It's relentless; the crusade to drive efficiency through every single process in the organization. When it comes to accounts payable most of the focus, with good reason, is on invoice processing. Lots of progress has been made in that regard. But processing invoices is only half the battle. Making the payment once the invoice has been approved and verified is another huge block of work, comprised of a number of steps. The possibility of improved efficiency in that regard should not be overlooked.

Cost cutting can be achieved in one of two ways:

1. You can make the process more efficient (reduce or eliminate manual processes that add little or no value) and/or
2. You can reduce costs

Let's take a look at ten tactics any organization can use to make their payment process either more efficient, more cost effective or both.

Efficiency Savings

When your process is more efficient, inherently, it saves the organization money. Here are a few strategies you can use to achieve that goal.

Tactic #1: Convert as many paper check payments to ACH as possible. Paper checks cost more than many people realize. It's not only the expense of the paper check, the envelope and the postage, but also the people costs associated with intensive manual processes. These expenses relate not only to the issuance of the checks but also the reconciliation and follow up on uncashed checks.

Tactic #2: Consider outsourcing check printing to your bank. At the end of the day, printing checks is not a core competency of any entity, except perhaps the banks. There is no reason to waste valuable, and expensive, human resources on it. Once you have the check issuance process down tight, turn the last steps over to the pros.

Tactic #3: If printing checks, do not take them to the mail room until right before the checks go to the post office. Taking checks to the mail room earlier increases the risk of check fraud since, in most organizations, there are numerous parties walking in and out of a mailroom all day.

Tactic #4: Move as many small dollar purchases to payment with p-cards instead of paper checks. Depending on how efficient your processes are, the cost to process an invoice can run anywhere from $5 to $50. Why are you spending this on invoices of low value? A better practice is to push all purchases below $100 or $500 to a card, assuming the seller accepts cards.

Tactic #5: If you are putting manual signatures on certain checks, consider raising the limit. Some organizations still insist on getting one or more manual signatures on paper checks over a certain dollar level. While this extra round of scrutiny (signers are supposed to review the backup before signing—otherwise the effort is wasted) may be warranted with extremely large payments, that is often not the case. If applicable, analyze the number of times signers actually find errors. Then review your review limits with an eye towards raising them—unless of course, your signers are finding errors.

Cost Cutting/Saving Measures

Taking a close look at the way you make payments, with an eye towards what each approach costs, you will find ways to cut costs without impacting the service provided regarding making payments.

Tactic #6: Replace wires with ACH, wherever possible. Wires are expensive and ACH is not. It's that simple. Keep in mind that there is no dollar limit on ACH transactions, although if you need same day settlement, the limit is currently $25,000 going to $100,000 on March 20,2020.

Tactic #7: Replace Rush wires with Same Day ACH, if under $25,009 ($100,000 after March 20, 2020. The newest option offered by banks for same day settlement removed the objection some had to ACH, if settlement is required on the same day.

Tactic #8: Replace checks delivered by expensive overnight delivery services with ACH. Overnight delivery service can be quite expensive, much more than ACH, even Same Day ACH. With either variety of ACH, the money is put directly into the vendor's bank account, saving them the trouble of having to take the check to the bank. The funds are also available immediately, unlike a check, which may have a short clearing period (of one or more days) before the bank allows use of the funds.

Tactic #9: Choose the most appropriate payment vehicle factoring in cost. So, while a purchase card might be appropriate for smaller payments, some vendors will balk at the suggestion that they take it for larger items. ACH is generally the preferred method of payment, if the vendor will accept it. The cost is low and there is no chance of it getting lost in the mail or bouncing. Checks, despite all their drawbacks, remain a popular choice in the United States while wires are frequently used for large international payments.

Tactic #10: If you have both a travel card and a p-card program, and are only getting a rebate on the p-card program, consider combining the two for a larger rebate. Also, if you have a fuel card program, consider adding that in to the mix, as well.

Concluding Thoughts

Not enough professionals give serious thought to reengineering their payment process with an eye towards making it more efficient and cost effective. Many simply take it for granted. They may shop around for the credit card program that offers the best rates and the highest rebate, but few steps back and look at what they are actually paying to make payments. Sometimes, as discussed above, there is another approach that costs less but yields the same result.

Now, to be fair, sometimes the payment process is tied to the banking arrangement and the company agreed to issue checks through a particular bank as part of its overall banking and financing needs. But that is not frequent.

By reviewing your current process, you may be able to take advantage of some of the tactics discussed in this piece and use them to create an equally effective but more efficient payment process for your organization.

Payments Made Outside Accounts Payable

Research by AP Now reveals that 80% of ACH payments are made by the accounts payable staff. This means that 20% not made in accounts payable. On the face of it this many not seem like a big problem. But, if organizations aren't careful about this issue, they could have a huge problem on their hands.

The Issue: The problem revolves around the controls used in accounts payable versus the ones used by other departments making payments. Consider the following questions.

- Are they employing the same tight internal controls and strong procedures used in accounts payable?
- Are they doing the 3-way match?
- Are they using rigid coding standards?
- Are they extinguishing the PO when the transaction is complete?
- Are they extinguishing the receiving document when the transaction is complete?
- Are they entering the invoice number correctly?

If they aren't and a second invoice shows up in accounts payable, it will be processed correctly and payment will be made. For if the PO and receiving documents are open, why shouldn't the processor make the payment? And, it is an unfortunate reality that vendors rarely return duplicate payments without some external encouragement. This means either having someone on staff look for duplicate payments or hiring a third-party auditor. Both are expensive options for a problem that could be eliminated through some simple training and processes.

Solution: In an ideal world we'd have all payments made in accounts payable to ensure uniformity in process and that proper controls and processes were used.

While this might be a recommended best practice, we want to go on record as stating we realize that if the organization is already having ACH payments made outside accounts payable, this is going to be a hard change to get approval for.

Probably a more realistic approach is to offer same training to group making ACH payments as is given to the accounts payable staff. If you explain reasoning in a calm and non-confrontational manner, you are likely to get concurrence from the other department. This means you have to be something of a salesperson, explaining why the fine points accounts payable insists on are so important.

Be forewarned that this will not be an easy task. Even if you get the manager of the other department to agree and the staff does attend your training, the odds are high that they will sometimes forget some of your pointers, like extinguishing an open receiver.

Considerations

More than occasionally, folks outside accounts payable don't fully grasp what can go wrong when best practices aren't followed. And, they certainly don't think about the financial implications. If your organization is one where payments are made outside accounts payable and best practices are not taken seriously, you will simply need to wait for something to go wrong.

This may seem terrible on the face of it, but it's the only way to make your point, the accounts payable version of "a picture's worth a thousand words."

When you find a problem (say a PO not extinguished) NICELY point it out. Even better, if an invoice shows up and is processed and you're able to identify it as one that was paid outside accounts payable, bring this to the attention of those making that ACH payment. If you have a payment audit done (and every organization should), see if they find duplicate payments as a result of proper procedures not being followed by the group making ACH payments. Share the documentation from the audit firm to make your point.

It is imperative that if you take this approach, you do so very tactfully avoiding pointing a fingers as much as possible. Make your points as diplomatically as you can choking back your instinct to say what's really on your mind.

Today's Reality

This is an issue that deserves serious consideration at those organizations moving away from paper checks and increase their electronic payments. Perhaps it is time to move the responsibility for making ACH payments back to accounts payable???

Chapter 10: Starting an ACH Program

As organizations everywhere start the move away from paper checks, ACH plays a critical role in that process. AP Now has long been an advocate of using the ACH as part of an effective payment program. That's probably why our editorial director was invited to give a workshop at the American Payroll Association's Annual Congress on Creating an Effective Payment Program. What follows is small part of her presentation on getting the most from your ACH program.

Why ACH?

For starters, ACH payments are among the most cost-effective payment mechanisms an organization has at its disposal. They are far cheaper than paper checks and create far fewer problems. The headaches associated with producing a paper check (signing, collating, mailing, lost checks etc.) are completely eliminated giving the accounts payable staff more time to focus on more value-added tasks.

An added benefit is the fact that there are no uncashed checks and hence no unclaimed property to follow up on, research, and report on.

Readers are cautioned against inviting any vendor to participate in an ACH program that might be targeted at a future date for participation in a p-card vendor. While vendors who are having trouble in a paper check world might be delighted to accept a p-card for payment, those who are being paid electronically will find your p-card program less attractive, given the discount they must give their card issuer.

Pricing Discounts

Occasionally, in certain industries, vendors interested in receiving electronic payments will offer a small pricing discount to those customers who pay in that fashion. Readers should be aware that this is different than the early payment discount. If this is a vendor from which your organization buys in large quantities the discounts, however small, will add up to a large dollar amount—money that goes straight to the bottom line.

If one vendor in a given industry offers pricing discounts, its competitors are likely to offer them as well—so ask if you are also buying from them. In fact, it doesn't hurt to ask any vendor that wants to be paid electronically if there is a pricing discount to be had.

Payment Terms

Many CFOs will insist that payment terms be renegotiated when an ACH program is started. This is because in an electronic payment world, float is eliminated. If the organization still pays on the initial payment date, the vendor in effect will have benefited by receiving the funds earlier than it would have in the paper check world. Typically, in these cases the float is split and two or three days are added to the payment terms.

Even if the vendor won't agree to the renegotiated terms, ACH still makes a lot of sense given the costs and hassle associated with creating paper checks.

When you move to ACH do not overlook the cash flow impact. In a paper check environment, checks will clear over a matter of days and occasionally longer. With ACH the cash hit is immediate. There is no delay as companies wait to go to the bank with their deposits. When you start a program make sure the treasurer or whoever is responsible for cash forecasting is aware of what you are doing.

No Doesn't Mean No Forever

Just because a vendor isn't capable of accepting electronic payments today doesn't mean it will never be able to accept them. Don't give up. Track the vendors you approach along with the reasons they give for not accepting electronic payments.

Then, periodically revisit the issue with them. We suspect after the difficulty some suppliers had in getting paid during the COVID-19 crisis, more than a few will be looking for ways to accept electronic payments. You might want to revisit the issue with any vendor who had payment issue.

Often a supplier will refuse to accept electronic payments but when a large customer draws a line in the sand demanding to pay with ACH, they makes the necessary changes to accommodate their customer. At that point you may be able to get the vendor to take payments electronically from your organization too. Of course, you won't be aware of the change so will need to continually touch base with your vendors.

Insist for Rush Payments

Advocate for management backing of a policy of all rush payments being made electronically. Not only does it save on the costs of producing the paper checks and overnight delivery costs but it also introduces another vendor to electronic payments.

Often all it takes is one payment for them to see how much easier electronics are. And if they are concerned about the remittance information, don't forget to send the details via e-mail.

Requisitioner Problem

If you are one of those organizations with a problem of requisitioners requesting the return of the printed check for delivery to the vendor—a really bad practice by the way—ACH provides an end run around it. Identify those vendors whose checks are regularly returned to the person who requested them rather than being mailed. Then target those organizations for your electronic payment program.

Once you have them on board, there will be no paper checks to return. Expect to have a row or two with the requisitioners involved—but if the vendor is happy with the process, they may end up getting on board with the program.

Don't Have an ACH Program?

Not every organization is paying via the ACH today—although the number who don't is dwindling rapidly. Some of the first calls AP Now got when the coronavirus crisis hit and AP teams were working remotely was, "how can I start an ACH program?" The answer is, "Call your bank and they will help you get set up."

Keep a list of every vendor who requests electronic payments. Then, when you finally get your program up and running, you'll have a group of vendors who are not only willing but also experienced.

ACH Primer: Credits, Debits – both Traditional and Same Day

With the sudden onslaught of interest in ACH from both businesses and unfortunately crooks, a review of the basics of how ACH works is in order. For without a thorough understanding of how these payment vehicles work, it is difficult for an organization to protect itself. We cannot underestimate the importance of understanding this payment tool as both users and non-users are at risk for various types of fraud if they do not take the appropriate steps. And then of course, there is the added benefit of ACH payments being a more efficient way to address invoices.

The Basics: ACH Credits

An ACH credit is a payer-initiated transaction. The payer instructs its financial institution to electronically transmit the payment through the ACH/Federal

Reserve network to the payee's bank account. Typically, the funds are available the day after the transaction takes place. This eliminates all delays associated with mail and processing float.

The most common examples of this are direct deposit of payroll, where the employer is the payer and the employee the payee. One of the biggest users of this type of payment vehicle is the Federal government when it direct deposits Social Security payments. In this case the recipients are the payees. It should be noted that starting in 2013, anyone signing up to receive Social Security benefits will have to receive them electronically. The Feds are starting to get out of the paper check business.

In recent years, businesses of all sorts have started making payments using the ACH instead of paper checks or in some cases, wire transfers. Because of the connection to direct deposit, this has led some to refer to this type of payment as a 'direct payment.'

The Basics: ACH Debits

An ACH debit is a payee-initiated transaction. The payee instructs the payer's financial institution to electronically transmit the payment through the ACH/Federal Reserve network to the payee's bank account. Typically, the funds are available the day after the transaction takes place. These transactions are initiated using your bank transit and routing number and your bank account number. It is implied that you have given your consent but there is no formal verification process by the bank to ensure you have given your approval. There are new bank products just emerging that provide some protection against unauthorized debits.

The most common examples of the use of ACH debits is in the financial services sector. Some financial institutions granting mortgages will, with the payer's permission, debit the payer's bank account for the agreed amount on an agreed upon date each month. Sometimes there is a slight reduction in the mortgage rate in exchange for this arrangement. The insurance industry has also used this approach with some of its insurance products.

This payment vehicle has also migrated to the business community. Some states collect their sales and use tax using this approach. A few organizations make intercompany transfers this way. In a couple of rare instances ACH debits are negotiated as part of the terms and conditions in a sales agreement. While we never expect to see ACH debits play a prominent part in the payment world, they are a vehicle that will play a continuing role. It is critical that every professional involved with payments understand them because they are used by fraudsters in growing numbers.

The Basics: Same Day ACH

Modernizing the US payment system in a manner that creates value for both the end users and the banks is one of the reasons for the move to same day ACH. Now, ACH transactions can settle next day (traditional) or Same Day. The limit on Same Day transactions is $100,000.

Starting an ACH Payment Program: What Better Time Than Now?

Without a doubt, at some point in the next decade, every organization will make at least part if not all of their payments electronically. Many have already started to do so. Others are considering programs now—or will be in the near future when an 800-pound-gorilla supplier insists on electronic payments. If you haven't yet started an electronic program, what follows is a look at some of the issues you should consider before launching one. Readers should note that they will sometimes hear ACH payments referred to as direct payments, a play on direct deposit of payroll.

Start with the Bank

The first place you need to go if you want to pay using ACH is to the bank where your checking account is. The bank officer assigned to your account should be able to put you in touch wit the right personnel in the bank. He or she will help you get set up and offer you some advice on converting vendors. Don't contact any vendor until you are comfortable with the process the bank suggests. You may have to make certain adjustments to your processes or accounting system and in all likelihood this will require technical support.

Depending on who has the relationship with the bank, it may be necessary to get treasury or accounting involved. Only when you have the banking, accounting, and IT concerns under control should you consider your first electronic payment.

Crawling before You Walk

A good way to get started, says a controller we spoke with, is to begin paying employee expense reimbursements by ACH. This will save money for the company (the cost of printing checks) and time for the employees (no need to make a trip to the bank to deposit reimbursement checks). Also, it will give the accounts payable department an opportunity to get used to the process. It should be an easy set up since payroll should have the direct deposit info on file so there is an opportunity to have a few "good wins" in the transition.

Once everyone is comfortable with the process, she advises, begin contacting your vendors and asking if it is possible to make payments electronically. This step should be taken with some care. Some who have contacted all their vendors at one time have learned the hard way— when the positive response was much higher than they anticipated—that they couldn't accommodate everyone at once.

The controller explains this can happen because most companies are happy to accept electronic payments, as it reduces their processing costs (no taking checks to the bank) and the funds received are verified (no bounced checks). ACH payments are typically free to receive, so they also avoid the processing costs charged by their bank and eliminate the "float".

The Cash Flow Impact

Our readers, warns the controller, should also consider that transitioning to ACH payments will have an impact on cash flow (no float) as the money will be withdrawn from their account typically within two days of initiating the transfer. Therefore, it's important that those doing cash flow forecasting be included in the ACH planning. More than one accounts payable manager has ended up with egg on his or her face after implementing what they thought was a great program only to have cash flow fall short of what was planned and management less than pleased with the outcome.

There is a relatively simple solution to this problem, although it will take some planning and management support. Many organizations renegotiate their payment terms to take an extra two or three days to make the transaction float neutral.

Auditors really like ACH payments, points out the controller, since there are no checks sitting around on someone's desk waiting to be mailed. She also notes that controllers are also happy due to fewer outstanding items on the bank reconciliation at the end of the month. Given the rough economic times many organizations currently face, do not down play the importance of cash flow.

Getting Vendor Information

An accounting manager we spoke with explained how he verifies bank information. "We require a copy of a cancelled check, a copy of a deposit ticket or ACH instructions on company letterhead maybe with an office signature to verify information," he says.

This step is taken to ensure that no one inserts their own bank information. Some organizations will only take the voided check or deposit ticket. The opportunity for fraud is high here, although to be honest there have only been a limited number of reports of this type of fraud.

Other Considerations

There are other issues to take into consideration when starting a program. They include:

- Be careful who you invite. If you have any thoughts of paying a particular vendor with a credit card in the future, do not invite them to participate in your program. It will be difficult to convert them from ACH to p-card, so better to avoid the issue completely.

- Depending on the accounting system in use, it may still be possible to do a separate "check run" in AP for electronic payments so that the record-keeping is easier. If the accounting system in use does not allow for this, then the reader should consider how these records will be kept.

- Consider creating a FAQ brochure for vendors answering the most common questions. This preemptive approach can help overcome objections before they occur.

- Once you have contacted all vendors, look for other ways to get vendors into your ACH program. One of the easiest is to insist that all rush payments will be made by ACH, not paper check. In many cases once they receive one payment electronically, they'll never want to go back to paper.

Concluding Thoughts

Whether or not you have a program now, electronic payments will play a big part in the payment world of the future. This is one of those areas everyone needs to learn about and master doing well.

What Can Go Wrong: Anticipate These Four ACH 'Gotchas' for ACH Success

Speeding up cash disbursements isn't an approach most organizations willingly adopt. It's even worse when the move is unexpected—something that somehow never happens when the organization is flush with cash. (It always seems to occur when cash is tight.) Yet, that is exactly what can happen when an organization moves from checks to ACH if they don't plan ahead and make the appropriate changes in payment terms. Whenever an organization makes a change in procedures, it is crucial that thought be given to all the ramifications; the move to ACH is no exception. AP Now recently asked readers of our ezine who've made the move to ACH what issues others should expect so they can avoid fallout.

Extinguishing POs and Receivers

One of the first issues that come to mind is a surprising metric. While most checks payments are made through accounts payable, the same cannot be said for ACH payments. In a good number of organizations ACH payments are also initiated in other departments.

A very real concern is that the other departments might not extinguish the POs and open receivers opening the organization to another potential avenue for duplicate payments. We believe if others are to make ACH payments, it's crucial that adequate training be provided to those individuals. Open POs and receivers can result in duplicate payments should a second invoice be presented.

Additionally, state auditors could construe the open receiver as unclaimed property. And, if you think this is something I'm making up, let me warn you that a few organizations are fighting with state auditors over this very issue right now. Should the auditors win, they will be looking at every organization's open receivers when they come for an audit.

Open receivers can cause a misstatement of your financial records if those receivers are used for accrual purposes. If there are enough of them, the misstatement could be material. This is something no one wants hanging over them.

Obviously, these issues are avoided if the organization insists that ACH payments must flow through the accounts payable system.

Setup Time Involved

"Our ERP software for the pay cycle was setup to create ACH files from these invoices but the output was nothing like what was required from the bank," reports an AP manager who requests anonymity. She notes that her staff spent endless hours completing the process to automate ACH payments. The company cut ACH payments for over 30 companies and all activity is now output to a file that is uploaded to its bank once a day. While the time savings once the process was in place is impressive, underestimating the time and effort needed to get the ACH process up and running can come back to haunt you.

This company was not home free once they had the process working, however. When they merged with another organization, they had to integrate their ACH payments with their new partners'. In this case the treasury department was involved and coordination became an issue.

Cash Flow Implications

Changing to ACH has a direct and immediate effect on cash flow. One way to compensate for the immediate disbursal of funds, she says, would be to extend your payments to vendors a few days longer. So, if you would normally cut a check on, say, May 16th wait until the 22nd to make the ACH payment. In fact, many organizations anticipate the cash flow impact and renegotiate terms with their vendors at the time they move to ACH. Those who ignore this issue will have a rude awakening the first time the ACH payments hit.

Depending on how tight the cash flow is in your organization, this could be the worst problem of all and the one with the highest visibility. If the company runs out of cash and the cause of the liquidity crisis is identified as the move to ACH without an accompanying renegotiating of payment terms, the results will not be pretty. This is not how any employee wants to come to the attention of upper management.

The Cash App Issue

The remittance advice can be problematic since there is no check stub for the vendor to see what invoices are being paid. Print off remittance advices and e-mails them to the vendors. You could mail it but the payment would arrive before the remittance advice. When vendors don't know how to apply payments, they call. And that adds more work to the accounts payable department partially offsetting the productivity gains from going electronic.

Finally, if the remittance advice is mailed, the postage cost savings goes up in smoke.

Keep in mind there are different methods of ACHing funds. With the Nach (National Automated Clearing House Association) PPD format you just send the payment and follow up with the details using another method of communication (like e-mail, fax, or mail of the remittance). However, with the CCD format you can send the details along electronically with the payment.

Concluding Thoughts

Use of the ACH for payment processes can result in significant savings for the organization. However, like any new process, if the full ramifications are not explored its implementation can make the process worse rather than better. By addressing the issues discussed above, you will be well on your way to avoiding an ACH implementation debacle.

ACH Payment Control Best Practice Checklist.

Don't let lack of controls derail your program. Make sure you include the following best practice internal controls.

Best Practice #1: Have detailed written procedures for your ACH program and include them in the accounts payable policy and procedures manual.

Best Practice #2: Make sure your ACH procedures mirror you check procedures.

Best Practice #3: Integrate strong internal controls throughout the process.

Best Practice #4: Check for duplicate payments made using other payment methodologies, i.e. paper check, T&E and p-card. Ideally every organization should be paid using one and only one payment mechanism.

Best Practice #5: Make sure receivers and POs are extinguished just as they would be if a paper check was the payment mechanism.

Best Practice #6: Put ACH blocks on all accounts where ACH activity will not be allowed. This is something every organization should do, regardless of its participation in the electronic payment arena.

Best Practice #7: Use ACH filters on those accounts where ACH debit activity will be allowed.

Best Practice #8: Have daily bank account reconciliations done on all accounts where ACH debits are permitted. Even better, reconcile all bank accounts on a daily basis.

Best Practice #9: Use a separate PC for all your online banking activities and do not use the computer for anything else.

Best Practice #10: Keep up to date on the latest information regarding fraud protection products offered by your financial institution and new frauds being perpetrated by crooks. They are getting amazingly creative.

Chapter 11: Expanding an ACH Program

Perhaps you've heard a lot about ACH recently and want to dip your foot into those waters. Or you're paying a few suppliers using the ACH and like the way it's going and want to add more vendors to your program. Or maybe you are just sick of the aggravation or paper checks. Or, in recent days, you've had a nightmare of a time getting suppliers paid while the AP team was in quarantine.

In growing numbers organizations everywhere are looking at ACH as a way to make their payment process more efficient. What follows is a plan that can be used by both those looking to get started as well as those who've taken a few tentative steps in the ACH payment arena.

Laying the Groundwork

Whether you're just beginning your investigation or have been paying a few vendors electronically, it is critical that you know what your bank capabilities are in this area. It is also important that you know what they require as well as what fraud detection and prevention services they offer. If you have them in for a meeting, it might be a good idea to also find out about their plans for the future in these areas.

Once you've got your banking facts in order, you will need to make the case to management. This includes, listing the benefits doing a financial analysis showing the cost savings as well as presenting what's available from the banking community.

You might also include any pitfalls you anticipate. This is critical because without a doubt, the process won't go smoothly. So make sure you include how you plan to address these potential issues. Then when they occur, everyone will be prepared. The problems might include:

1) Pushback from staff who are used to do everything a certain way and will have to learn a new way.

2) The impact on cash flow when all payments hit on the first day instead of being spread out over a week or so. You can renegotiate payment terms to address this issue and make it cash flow neutral.

3) Initially, you will not be able to reduce staff associated with the payment function as the personnel who normally handled your paper checks will be busy working to get vendors set up on your new payment program. Eventually you will be able to shift personnel to more value added work.

Not only do you need to convince management to convert as many payments to ACH as possibly, ideally you want to get at least one executive onboard in a big way. That way, when those inevitable complaints start appearing, you'll have someone in your corner to insist that the program move forward.

The First Date

Expect that the first few times you pay electronically it will go less than smoothly. This is normal. You need to try the program to work out whatever unexpected kinks there are in the process. If you are lucky, they will be minor. But don't hold your breathe. Assume the worst and that way you'll either be pleasantly surprised or at least not disappointed.

Given your low expectations you will want to select your test group carefully. Do not include the vendor who complains about everything no matter how much they insist. Rather choose a few vendors who are easy to work with. You might include vendors who have requested electronic payments or those who you have captive relationships with, for example subsidiaries. Practice on friends and family, so to speak, before taking your show on the road.

After your first set of transactions, review what happened and identify any problems or rough spots. Reengineer your procedures to address these complications before your second set of transactions. Only when you are certain that the process is running smoothly are you ready to roll out your program to a larger audience.

The Big Rollout

Once you've gotten your feet wet and ironed out any problems in your program, you are ready to introduce your new payment program to your vendor community. You probably want to proceed piecemeal because it does take some time to enroll each vendor. One company ended up with egg on its face after sending a solicitation to all its vendors. It got a much higher response than expected and could not get everyone on board quickly. This resulted in disgruntled vendors which was not the response they were hoping for.

A better approach might be to send a solicitation to about one-quarter of your vendors. This might include anyone who has asked about electronic payments as well as those who are sending their invoices to you electronically. These groups will probably be most receptive.

Once you've enrolled everyone from the group that shows interest, approach another group of vendors. Based on the response rate from the first group, you'll be able to figure out how big your second solicitation should be.

After each group, review the process and identify any new problems that may have cropped up. Ideally there will be none, but that is not a safe assumption.

The Hardcore Holdouts

Eventually you will have approached all your vendors. However, there will still be some who have not taken advantage of your offer, no matter how attractive it is. At that point a corporate decision needs to be made regarding how hard to push this issue.

Some organizations accept the fact that not everyone wishes to be paid electronically. Others push the issue. For example, Social Security is mandating a move to electronic payments. This is what it says on its website:

Other organizations have decreased the frequency of their check runs while increasing the frequency they make ACH payments to encourage vendors to take payments electronically.

The Remittance Information

One of the reasons some companies are reluctant to accept electronic payments is their ability to apply cash. Without the remittance information that typically accompanies a paper check, they are hard pressed to apply cash correctly. You can address this concern. The simplest solution is to email the appropriate Accounts Receivable person at the vendor with the information that would typically go on the remittance advice.

Talk to your IT folks to see if they can help you devise a solution to this issue. You might also want to discuss it with your bankers when you have that preliminary meeting with them. They may be able to share with you how some of their other customers addressed this problem.

Don't Rest on Your Laurels

Once you've got the program up and running smoothly, don't rest. Stay on top of advancements in the payment arena to identify ways to improve your current process. Also, make sure you continue to monitor the fraud situation both to understand both the new frauds occurring as well as the tools being developed by the financial community to fight those scams.

And finally, don't forget to periodically calculate the savings your electronic payment program is delivering to the organization. This is money that goes right to the bottom line. Make sure management is aware of this contribution made by an improvement to the accounts payable process.

How Companies Are Growing ACH Programs

The benefits of making payments electronically rather than paying with a paper check are many— both for the purchaser and the seller. Yet paper checks continue to be used, most notably in the US. In a recent AP Now Payments survey, we asked professionals responsible for payments in the US how they were convincing their suppliers to accept ACH payments.

What follows is a quick look at the four most common methods and then a longer discussion of 20 less-common, but quite innovative, methods currently in use.

Commonly-Used Converting Techniques

AP Now asked those who said they were interested in growing their electronic payment program about the strategies they were using. They were invited to check all strategies being used so the totals will exceed 100%. Here's what they said they were doing:

- Reach out to vendors in an organized manner encouraging them to accept. This approach is used by 46% of the survey respondents.

- Do nothing! This approach is used by 34% of the survey respondents.

- Pay anyone electronically who asks but have no formal program   . This approach is used by 19% of the survey respondents.

- Offer to pay vendors faster if they accept electronic payments. This approach is used by 15% of the survey respondents.

- Mandate usage for targeted purchases. This approach is used by 9% of the survey respondents.

That's right over one-third indicated they wanted to expand their electronic payments program but were doing nothing to accomplish that goal.

Innovative Less-Commonly Used Approaches

As part of this survey, respondents shared other techniques they used to convince their suppliers to accept electronic payments. Let's take a look at some of them.

- Many organizations start their electronic payment expansion program with their expense report reimbursements. They mandate that all reimbursements for employee expense expenses go through the ACH process. While it is not legal in many states to mandate the use of electronic payments for payroll, you can do so for business travel reimbursements

- While it would be nice if you could convert every vendor in one fell swoop, that is not realistic. Invite a handful of vendors at a time to participate in ACH. When they have been successfully onboarded and you have adjusted your process for any hickups you encountered, move onto the next group. Gradually you will increase the number getting paid in this manner.

- Take an aggressive stance with new vendors. Upon onboarding vendors, tell them the only payment option is ACH. Very few will object. Most will simply provide their banking information. This means you don't have to have the conversation with them, try and convince them of the benefits or otherwise spend time that could be better used for something else.

- Make sure information about accepting ACH payments is everywhere your vendors might look. Work with product folks to put ACH application link as part of welcome packet. You might also mention it prominently in your welcome letter and annual letter to vendors. If you have a password protected intranet site for your vendors, include it there. Unfortunately, if your vendor information is not in a protected place and open to the public, it is a better idea not to include your information there. If you do, fraudsters will see it and you may increase your chances of being attacked by a crook trying to defraud your organization. Don't help them.

- Make it easier to get paid with ACH. Limit the number of check runs over time. You might start with one check run a week and three ACH runs. Then lessen payments by check to twice a month and then to once a month. When a vendor complains simply point out that they could bet paid faster if they accepted electronic payments.

- Make converting suppliers a team effort. Get procurement involved. Make sure they understand how important it is to get away from paper checks. Ask them if they will make electronic payments an option during contract negotiations.

- With every paper check mailed, include an insert that explains to vendors the benefits of accepting electronic payments if they provide banking information. Tell them what they have to do to convert to electronic payments. Make the process as simple as possible for them. This will have limited success as many don't read the inserts with checks. But, it won't cost much.

- Working with purchasing, adjust payment terms to match the payment method used. For example, contact your vendors and offer them a credit card payment with Net 1 terms, or an ACH payment with Net 25 terms or paper checks with terms of Net 30 or even Net 45. Eventually you may be able to extend terms on paper checks to Net 60.

- Make payment by ACH the default method for newly added suppliers. If they want paper checks they have to opt out. Those who take this approach find that very few do; most stay with the electronic payments.

- Insist that all rush payments will be made by ACH. If it is a rush and the vendor wants a paper check, they have to wait for the next check run. Most will take the electronic payment under these circumstances. Hopefully, once they are paid this way one time, they will recognize the convenience and practicality of the approach.

Concluding Thoughts

Electronic payments are the wave of the future. The economics of using them is overwhelming. The faster you can convert the majority of your payments to them, the more efficient and effective your payment process will be.

When looking on what approaches you want to take, be innovative. Combine several of the above approaches, with the ultimate goal of converting 100% of your vendors to electronic payments. Begin during the vendor onboarding process. Your form can state that ACH is your method of payment. You can process ACH payments daily while reducing the number of check runs. This automatically extends terms for suppliers receiving checks.

Don't be like the 34% mentioned at the beginning who want to expand their electronic payment program but are doing nothing. Use some of the techniques discussed here to rid your suppliers of their paper check addiction. You'll be doing them a favor.

20 Tested Ways to Encourage Vendors to Accept ACH Payments

Less than 50% of B2B payments in the US are made electronically. There are far too many paper checks clogging up the payment process. What follows are tactics used by our readers to improve this situation. One of more should help your organization in its battle to minimize paper payments.

1. Offer more favorable terms to those accepting ACH payments than those insisting on paper checks. This is typically done by reducing the number of check runs slowly over time.

2. During the new vendor onboarding process, request that the vendor provide information that will permit you to pay them with ACH.

3. Whenever there is correspondence with a supplier about any accounts-payable-related issue, ask if they would like to receive ACH payments.

4. Use check stuffers touting the benefits of receiving ACH payments and directing them where to sign up.

5. When mailing check payments to the vendor include an ACH form for them to complete.

6. Create an annual mailing sent to all suppliers currently receiving checks requesting updated information and asking them to move to ACH or Credit Card payments.

7. Require ACH payments to vendors who offer a prompt pay discounts.

8. Enlist the help of a third party to help onboard suppliers to ACH payments.

9. We are transitioning to making ACH payments a contractual obligation.

10. Require an ACH form to be filled out at the time the vendor is set up.

11. The Vendor ACH sign up form is provided at the time the vendor is established. ACH is noted as the preferred method of payment in contracts.

12. Periodically (every few months) send a colored buck slip and Authorization form with checks to remind suppliers of your ability to pay them via ACH. By using a brightly colored piece of paper you stand a better chance of having it read. Use a different color each time.

13. Automatically sign vendors up to receive ACH credits if they include their ACH payment information on their invoice. Verify with a phone call before setting up in our system.

14. Take the opportunity to discuss ACH when a vendor calls to complain that a check payment hasn't been received. You can use this call to let them know they will receive their payments faster and this will lessen the chance of certain frauds.

15. Include the information needed to make ACH payments on your Supplier Data Sheet. When the information isn't received ask the Purchasing Department to obtain the information from the vendor.

16. Discourage new vendors from check payments by requesting their electronic payment information at the beginning of the relationship.

17. Offer longer pay terms if the supplier wants a check and explain this to them. One company reports extending payment terms to Net 50 days for checks.

18. Your welcome package should include the request for information to pay invoices electronically.

19. Make electronic payment a requirement for all new vendors

20. Provide the ACH form up front and do not offer other forms of payment for domestic suppliers

How AP Now Readers Convinced More Suppliers to Sign up for ACH Payments

The reasons for switching from paper checks to ACH payments are many. Cost, efficiency, minimization of unclaimed property issues and cash flow planning are just a few. Despite the recognized benefits to both parties, there is still some reluctance by many suppliers to accept electronic payments. We recently asked readers of our weekly e-zine who've been successful getting vendors to sign up for ACH how they persuaded them to do so. Here's a few of the better suggestions.

The Payment Frequency Issue

Perhaps the best way to get vendors on board is to pay less frequently with checks than with ACH. That's the strategy used by quite a few of our readers. Here are a few of their comments on implementing this tactic.

- To encourage ACH, checks were cut only twice monthly whereas we did ACH daily.

- Have quicker payment terms for those vendors that accept ACH payments.

- We encourage our vendors to give us a discount and be paid by ACH. We pay these vendors on a daily basis. Otherwise, they are paid once per week.

The Benefits Approach

Quite a few companies convince vendors by simply pointing out the benefits. Here's how a few or our readers addressed the issue.

- We just let them know that by accepting ACH payments, they get paid faster and with more accuracy. No more checks lost in the mail, having to void and re-issue checks, no more phone calls from vendors looking for check payments and being told they are in the mail. ACH are easier to provide proof of payment and to validate taking early pay discounts.

- We have stressed that the time it will take for the vendor to actually receive funds will be decreased by at least a week. Between mailing the checks, taking the deposit to the bank and waiting for the check to clear. If we send an ACH, they will have funds in their account within two business days.

- We were struck by a major tornado last April. Our facilities were not impacted but unfortunately several of our vendors' physical locations were. In addition to that, during the days after the tornado, mail service was slow, if available at all in some locations. Fortunately, many of our vendors had previously signed up for ACH and we were able to continue making payments to them during this difficult time. We have been able to use this as a "plus" for ACH to convince vendors who were not signed up for ACH to do so.

The Lost Checks Opportunity

A number of readers took advantage of checks lost either in the mail or by vendors to press for ACH. Here's a look at how a few of them handle the matter.

- We charge a replacement fee for lost checks unless the vendor has submitted an ACH request for future checks.

- Whenever a vendor calls to have a check voided and re-issued, we send them a form to sign up for ACH.

- Our company doesn't replace lost checks unless the vendor submits an ACH request.

A Helping Hand from Purchasing

Increasingly accounts payable's activities overlap with other departments, especially purchasing. Here's how two of our readers recruited other departments to help.

- We encouraged the purchasing department, travel, premises (anyone engaging vendors to put ACH on the table as part of their negotiations). We managed to get some nice discount terms in the bargain.

- One of the strategies that our AP department implemented involves working in conjunction with our contracting team so that when it is time to renew our vendor price agreements, switching to electronic payment is part of the new contract.

Addressing the Remittance Information Issue

One of the biggest problems with getting vendors on board with electronic payments has to do with getting them the remittance information. Here's how two of our readers addressed that problem.

- Our company has a website where all the payments are posted (for a 3 year time frame) and the website also sends an auto email when the vendor has received a payment.

- Ask for an email address where remittance information can be sent.

Additional Strategies

Even after everything discussed, there are still a few more approaches being used by our readers. The first addresses vendor complaints about early discount payments received after the discount date and the second addresses the issue with new vendors. Here are the last two suggestions.

- We have some discount vendors still receiving checks. They will contact us requesting a discount be paid back because the check was not received in time. Our comment to this is we have no control over the mail time and suggest they switch to ACH. Allowing us to pay them by ACH they will receive our payments quicker and we will no longer have a late payment issue with discounts.

- Create a form that you can email over to all new vendors with their w9. See the sample of this form on page x. Readers should verify information received on this form using contact information provided by the vendor.

Paying via the ACH is the wave of the future. It is much easier and less costly than paper checks. If you are looking for ways to increase participation (or get started) some of our proven reader tactics may be just what you need.

Derailing the ACH Program: Payments Made outside Accounts Payable

While wires in many companies have always been made outside accounts payable, traditionally they were the only payments not made by the accounts payable staff. Since the items covered by wires were usually pretty easy to identify, the chances of a duplicate payment slipping through were not high, assuming the organization took a few basic steps to protect itself.

The advent of ACH is changing that situation. They are cheaper than both wire transfers and paper checks and appear to be the wave of the future for corporations making payments. Approximately, 20% of all organizations have ACH payments initiated outside of accounts payable. Since the items being paid by ACH are the same as the items being paid by the accounts payable staff, problems can arise under a few circumstances. If the outside staff does not use the same strong rigid controls used by accounts payable, duplicate payments will arise. Specifically, this means the staff outside accounts payable must:

     1) use the same rigid coding standards used in accounts payable;

     2) perform the three-way match; and

     3) extinguish purchase orders and receivers once the payment has been made.

If they do not follow the same standards, and an invoice appears in accounts payable, it will be paid, for the staff will have no way of knowing it had already been addressed. Thus, it is imperative that those organizations making payments outside accounts payable sufficiently train the staff making those payments so duplicates don't slip through.

Chapter 12: ACH Debit Best Practices

Because ACH debits are not used that frequently in the US at the current time and they were a recommended practice during the COVID-19 crisis, we thought we'd take a little space to focus on them.

To recap, An ACH debit is a payee-initiated transaction. The payee instructs the payer's financial institution to electronically transmit the payment through the ACH/Federal Reserve network to the payee's bank account.

Typically, the funds are available the day after the transaction takes place, unless it is Same Day. These transactions are initiated using your bank transit and routing number and your bank account number. It is implied that you have given your consent but there is no formal verification process by the bank to ensure you have given your approval. There are new bank products just emerging that provide some protection against unauthorized debits.

The most common examples of the use of ACH debits is in the financial services sector. Some financial institutions granting mortgages will, with the payer's permission, debit the payer's bank account for the agreed amount on an agreed upon date each month. Sometimes there is a slight reduction in the mortgage rate in exchange for this arrangement. The insurance industry has also used this approach with some of its insurance products.

In the B2B space, ACH debits are used most frequently for the payment of sales and use tax and the movement of money from a subsidiary to a parent.

ACH Debit Bet Practice

Do you allow ACH debits on some of your accounts? A small but growing number of organizations do. Those that do typically follow a two-pronged approach to ensure no fraudulent transactions get through. First, they provide their bank with information about the parties permitted to debit their accounts. This might be critical vendors who insist on it, some taxing authorities, and a few other parties such as utilities. Some organizations take this approach one step further and put a dollar limit on the amount allowable.

Even with these tight controls in place, it is recommended that the daily ACH debit activity be reviewed carefully to ensure no unauthorized debit slips through. Businesses have a very short-time frame in which to reject an unauthorized debit. So, this daily review is crucial to recovering funds taken inappropriately without a battle.

ACH Debit Fraud Protection Best Practice

One of the fastest growing payment frauds revolves around unauthorized ACH debits. Everyone is advised to put blocks on all accounts where ACH debit activity will not take place. For most organizations this means there will be one or two accounts where the debit activity will be directed. If your bank offers a filtering product and you only allow a handful of organizations to debit your account, you can give the bank that list and ask them to monitor the activity.

But what if your bank doesn't offer a filtering product? Or, what protection do you have that an approved vendor will not debit the account for an amount you did not agree to? Your best protection in either of these instances is to reconcile the account every single day. By taking that approach, you can notify the bank the moment you see an unauthorized charge.

Yes, this is a lot of work and something that tends to get back burnered when other chores piles up. But it's a task that should not be ignored. Missing one unauthorized debit could end up costing your organization millions.

ACH Fraud Protection: Bank Products Currently Available

Electronic payment fraud is nasty, unsettling and expensive. What's more, every organization is a potential target, regardless of whether they make electronic payments or not. Some think, "oh, we don't participate in that arena so we're safe." That is categorically not true. What's more, organizations who are hit with an unauthorized debit have only 24 hours to alert their banks. Otherwise, they have no recourse. As the sophisticated crooks involved in electronic payment fraud crank into high gear, it is more important than ever that every professional take the appropriate steps to protect their organization. The banks can help as well. This is a look at what's currently available from the banking community.

Background

Before we discuss the products available now and being introduced this year, it is important that readers understand they need to read the product descriptions very closely. Unfortunately, it is not like positive pay (at least currently) where we can say one name and everyone knows what the product does.

Read the product description and make sure it does what you think it does. Also, make sure you understand what, if any, your obligations are regarding the use of the bank product.

Bank Products

Currently, there are four types of products either available or very close to being available. They are:

1) ACH Blocks. These are instructions given a bank to block ACH activity. You can either have all ACH activity blocked or just ACH debit activity. This needs to be done on an account by account basis. What many organizations do if they want or need to allow ACH debits is to limit that activity to one or two accounts. They then put ACH blocks on all the other accounts. If you do not want to allow any ACH debit activity, put an ACH debit block on the account.

2) ACH Filters. Should you allow ACH debits on one or more accounts, you can put a filter in place. This is a list of organizations that you have given permission to debit your account. The bank often won't check the dollar amount, just the entity debiting your account. If they initiate an unauthorized transaction, the filter won't catch it. But the filter is a big step

in the right direction. New advances in this product area include enhancements like filtering for dollar amount and filtering for frequency of debits.

The first two products are currently available and most financial institutions offer them. The next two products are just starting to find their way into the marketplace. If your bank hasn't offered them to you, call them and ask about it.

3)   ACH Payee File. This is similar to the ACH filter, but works when you initiate the payment. With this product, you supply the bank with a list of entities and people you intend to pay using ACH. Then when your list of payments comes through, if there is a payment to an entity not on your preauthorized list, the payment will not be made. This product helps protect your organization against losses from an account takeover.

4)   Notification of ACH Debits. With this product, any time an ACH debit hits your account, the bank notifies you and asks if it should honor the transaction. Now, if this seems like a lot of work, consider this. Most organizations only allow a few entities to initiate ACH debits against their account. Hence, the number of phone calls should be small – unless a crook is trying to debit your account and you want those calls.

Concluding Thoughts

Whether we like it or not, ACH fraud continues to grow. What's more the crooks who focus on it are very sophisticated and they are continually devising new ways to steal from organizations just like yours. Thus, the protections that work today, may not address the problems that emerge next week or next year. So, it is imperative that once you create the perfect protection plan, you don't rest on your laurels. Continue to monitor the fraud situation.

Bank products are just one facet of the way we deal with the problem. Make sure you take advantage of what's out there.

Chapter 13: Expanding a Card Program

As organizations of all types and sizes look to improve the efficiency of their payment programs, p-cards stand out as a serious solution. P-cards are also sometimes referred to as corporate procurement cards or procurement cards. Not only are they a great way to handle the slew of small-dollar invoices that pour into every accounts payable department but their use helps track spend and monitor compliance. And then, of course, there is the issue of rebates.

Recharged Education's Lynn Larson is a frequent and popular speaker on p-card topics and growing your p-card program. She advocates the following strategies to help managers who want to expand the use of p-cards within their payment matrix.

Tactic 1. Combine travel in the program. A growing number of organizations are taking the "one-card" approach incorporating travel into their p-card programs. The most popular reason for incorporating travel is to grow the rebate. Since the items are already being paid for with a charge card, it is sometimes easy to adopt this approach.

If you choose this tactic, carefully analyze the impact on the accounting process as well as on the organization's travel policy.

In addition to the one-card approach already discussed, Larson makes some points about payroll cards and project cards.

- Payroll cards contain an available balance for use and are tied to the actual dollars earned by an employee, such as wages, benefits, or some type of expense reimbursement.

- Project cards are for a specific undertaking. Limits can be set to include a maximum-dollar amount and time limit. Limits can decline as the card is used until time or the credit is depleted.

These p-card variants may not be simple to implement and could require reengineering of processes, personnel etc. She notes that other expansion methods are likely to be easier to implement and she recommends that professionals first pursue the untapped potential within standard p-card programs.

Tactic 2. Increase the number of cardholders. This can be achieved by expanding the program into parts of the organization that currently do not have p-cards. She also suggests that some organizations will be able to increase penetration by simply giving the card to everyone who should have one.

Some firms are overly cautious when issuing cards. A careful study of who is purchasing what can sometimes uncover individuals who have not been included in the program but who should be. But proceed with care. Larson warns against over-distributing the cards. There is a fine line between too few and too many; carefully determine exactly when to stop expanding the number of people in the program.

Tactic 3. Convert more suppliers to p-card payments. Larson recommends beginning by reviewing company spend data from the AP system for non-p-card vendors to identify supplier opportunities. Once the potential suppliers have been identified, they can be approached.

Determine if the vendor in question already accepts credit cards. If so, the task has just gotten a lot simpler. Getting them on the p-card program might be as easy as notifying them that you wish to change your method of payment.

The identified suppliers not currently accepting cards will have to be educated. This is a more difficult task. She says the education process should be started by explaining the benefits of the program. Tell them how they will benefit.

Tactic 4. Increase the types of purchases included in the program. Look at the inventory purchases your company makes. Consider if there is an automated inventory in place. If there is, evaluate how a p-card payment integration would affect the process.

Larson suggests looking at capital equipment purchases. She warns listeners that including the p-card may require technology enhancements such as a new interface to the fixed-asset system.

A few companies include large ticket items, such as utility bills, phone bills, and maintenance agreements. Why? Because it impacts the revenue sharing (rebates) opportunities with the card provider.

A number of companies integrate their e-procurement systems with the p-card. Larson alerts companies that do this to consider:

- The type of p-card used (individual, ghost etc);

- The integration requirements with the e-procurement system and/or GL; and

- Reconciliation requirements.

She also suggests it might be possible to pay meeting expenses, temp labor, some consultants, catering, and training with a p-card.

Caveats

When expanding a program, especially when increasing the types of purchases, there may be implications to other departments. They should be included in the planning process. Specifically, there may be:

- Accounting implications;

- Additional technology requirements;

- Interface issues;

- Process changes that affect staff; and

- Data requirements.

Before getting started on your expansion plan, Larson warns that there is no on-size-fits-all solution. Readers can evaluate Larson's suggestions to identify missed opportunities and use some of the methods discussed to compose a plan to work within their own organization's unique constraints.

Test Tactics to Increase P-card Activity

P-cards are attractive to companies for a number of reasons including the fact that they get small-dollar invoices out of the invoice process, ultimately making the accounts payable department more efficient. As rebates become more commonplace, even for mid-size programs, the drive to increase usage within the organization intensifies. But, this doesn't mean haphazardly putting all possible purchases on the card. Rather a more reasoned approach needs to be taken.

Whether you are looking to increase usage because you want a higher rebate or you are simply looking to get some of those low-dollar invoices out of your invoice processing cycle is irrelevant. The techniques are the same. A few savvy companies have realized they can also improve their cash flow by using p-cards. They simply wait until the end of the payment cycle and then instead of paying with a check or ACH, they call up and provide their credit card information.

Here are a few ways best practice organizations have increased p-card usage in their organizations.

- Make sure everyone who has a card is using it every place they should be.

- Mandate the use; don't give employees an option.

- Educate every cardholder about all the potential opportunities to use the p-card.

- Increase the number of merchants in the p-card program

- Look for new opportunities to use the card. This can include things like paying for subscriptions, office supplies, and so on.

- Offer cards to all employees who make frequent small-dollar purchases.

- Whenever an invoice comes in that could have been paid for with a p-card, sending it back to the approver asking it be paid for with the p-card.

- With management support, refuse to pay any invoice with a check for which a p-card could be used.

- Consider merging your travel card and your fuel card into your p-card program.

Why P-card Programs Fail.

Do you wonder why you bother to have a p-card program? Is so little put on the cards each month that it doesn't seem worth the effort? If that is the case consider the following:

1. Have you given cardholders adequate training? Do they know where and when they are supposed to use the cards?

2. Is your program too restrictive? Have you set the limits too low or limited where and when the cards can be used?

3. Have you mandated use of the cards in those situations where you want employees to use the cards – or is it left to the employees' discretion?

By addressing these three basic issues you may identify the roadblock to your organization's p-card success.

Inactive P-cards

The best practice policy regarding the issuance of p-cards is to give them to everyone who has a business need for one and not to one other person. The business need has nothing to do with title or rank and everything to do with job responsibilities. Sometimes the two get mixed up and cards end up on the wallets of people who never use them. This is just an added risk that no company needs.

But how can you determine who needs them and who doesn't? The answer is actually rather simple. Periodically, say once a quarter, have your card issuer run a report showing all inactive cards. These cards may belong to people who have left the company. If after you do a little research, you determine that is the reason for the lack of activity, cancel those cards immediately. But what to do with those that are with employees who don't use them?

Have a quick conversation and find out if they really need the card or not. If they don't very tactfully request that the card be returned and canceled. If you determine that is not a politically smart move on your part, consider this action. When the card expires and the bank sends new cards, don't give these individuals the new cards. You can then cancel them. If at a later date, the person wants a card and a determination is made that they should have one, simply have the bank issue them a card at that time.

Don't Let Employees Share P-cards

Occasionally, organizations let several employees share one card rather than issue them to those who might only occasionally need them. This penny-wise-pound-foolish approach is just that—foolish. And when you look at it from an internal controls standpoint, sharing cards stands out as a phenomenally bad idea. We suspect that more than a few companies may have taken this shortcut during the COVID-19 crisis. If you did, make sure you put an end to it immediately. Also, double and triple check the transactions on the card.

If you think sharing cards wouldn't happen in your organization, consider whether any departments share a card because no one purchases enough to warrant their own—or so the reasoning goes. Please note: This is different than using ghost cards where the vendor has one card for the entire organization and that card is used for purchases with that vendor alone. In those cases the vendor should be responsible for tracking who made what purchase.

The reason why a card should not be shared is simple. As Gee explained, with several users the organization loses the single point of accountability and increases the possibility for fraud. Since no one can tell who made the charge, it's hard to assign responsibility.

Even if fraud isn't the issue, people can be quite absentminded and by the time the bill comes in the purchaser will have completely forgotten that they even used the card. Of course, in these situations the receipt is bound to be long gone.

The use of a single card for multiple employees also leaves open the issue of who is responsible for seeing that all of the charges are properly allocated. And, of course, if there is a mistake in an allocation there could be finger pointing when it comes to resolution. It doesn't take much thought to begin to identify the problems that could arise—and they far outweigh the small benefit of not issuing a few extra cards. What first appeared has a no-brainer winner of an idea to save a few dollars may turn out to be a big fat loser.

Cards Aren't Used after An Employee Leaves

While no one likes to talk about it, the fact is that employees do leave either of their own volition or by invitation. Often as the company scrambles to cover its operational bases making sure that former employee's tasks are covered, the T&E card given to the employee for company business is forgotten. And, let's face it, if the employee leaves with a bad taste in his or her mouth, leaving that card in his or her possession can be tempting fate.

Mostly this issue will apply to those companies who provide their employees with a T&E card. Employees should be instructed to turn in their cards as part of their exit process. In fact, if human resources conducts an exit interview or goes through a process where it gets back keys and employee ID cards, it can be instructed to also get back the T&E card.

But getting the card back is just a small part of the solution. The most important part is canceling the card with the bank. For if the bank isn't notified, the employee can simply write down the card number, expiration date and the three or four digit code. They can then go shopping to their heart's delight online and you'll have an awful time trying to get reimbursed.

Otherwise, in a small percentage of the cases, there will be a problem. This will occur when the employee uses the card for personal expenses. To a lesser extent the problem can occur if the employee was given a cash advance and never accounted for the funds, and/or perhaps never spent them on company business. (As cash advances continue to become less common, the cash-advance problem will become less and less of an issue.)

For starters, as part of the T&E as well as the employee manual, employees should be told that T&E cards need to be returned to the company when they depart. They also need to be informed that it is expected they will submit approved T&E reports for all company travel before they depart.

This is all fine and dandy when the parting is amicable. But occasionally it is not. Human resources should inform accounts payable or whoever is responsible for the T&E card program whenever an employee is fired. The cards of departing employees, whether fired or leaving of their own volition, should be terminated immediately. It is imperative that HR notify the card administrator in a timely manner so they can call the bank.

Internal Controls around Your Commercial Card Program

While companies might wish to increase spend on the card, the spend that should be going there should be legitimate spend. To that end, good controls around the card program are critical.

As part of the recent Internal Controls in Accounts Payable survey, policies around commercial card programs were examined. Robust controls for a commercial card program (e.g., p-cards) include properly preparing participants for their respective roles, as well as applying appropriate controls to the card program itself.

Participant Controls

These might include:

- Cardholders must use their cards as directed, reconcile their transactions, supply the required supporting documentation, and uphold security measures. They are the first line of defense against external fraud.

- Managers provide oversight, fulfilling an approver role. They must ensure cardholders adhere to the card program policies and procedures. They should specifically look for any signs of internal fraud.

Because both roles are so important, best practice organizations require cardholders **and** their manager-approvers to sign an "internal agreement" that outlines their respective responsibilities and states possible consequences for non-compliance. Yet, per the 2019 AP Now's Internal Controls in Accounts Payable, only 27% follow this. It is most common to only require cardholders to sign an internal agreement. This is an easy-enough practice to implement.

Delving deeper into the manager-approver role, it is a best practice to mandate that they are at least one functional job level higher than the cardholders whose transactions they review/approve. Again, data from the Internal Controls in AP Survey reveals that over half do enforce such a requirement. Another 20% indicated that they do this most of the time, allowing for the occasional exception.

Program Controls

The survey addressed six types of controls to apply to the cards in order to minimize inappropriate purchases and help prevent fraud. Let's take a look at the utilization of some of these controls.

- Monthly/cycle spend limits: 80%

- ATM/Cash blocks: 59%

- Per purchase/transaction limit: 50%

- MCC block: 48%

- Country block: 12%

- Limits on # of transactions allowed: 12%

As you can see, the survey results indicate that most organizations

under-utilize card controls. While not all will be applicable to all organizations, most will be. At an absolute minimum, ATM/cash access should be blocked, yet only 59% report doing this.

Use of Controls

When you look through the list of the more basic controls as presented in the list above, it is readily apparent that they are not complicated or that difficult to implement. Surely, most organizations must be using most of them? Alas that is not the case. Only 16% are using five or six of the aforementioned controls. Just over half are using three or four and one-third are using only one or two.

While it is true that some of the controls might not be appropriate in all situations, the numbers reveal a startling weakness in most existing card programs. For example, assuming that all your employees are honest and wouldn't take cash from an ATM using their card, will eventually lead to trouble. Whether the employee is disgruntled or has their back to the wall due to financial difficulties is irrelevant. Don't leave that door opened.

How good are the controls around your program? Might there be room for improvement on this front?

Chapter 14. Card Issues Created or Exacerbated by the COVID-19 Crisis

The COVID-19 crisis has spawned new problems while exacerbating old ones when it comes to corporate cards. Based on conversations with those providing services to the card community as well as end users, the following three issues have emerged:

- Cards Mailed during Quarantine
- Cards and Terminated Employees
- Deceitful Use of Cards for Personal Gain

Those additional issues that straddle the expense reporting topic will be discussed in the next chapter.

Issue #1: Cards Mailed during Quarantine

The COVID-19 crisis has spawned new problems for those mailing corporate cards. If the cards are to replace expiring cards of active users, then it is mandatory that they find their way into the hands of the users in a timely fashion. However, several problems have arisen in this regard. For starters, the mail is being returned from some organizations, if they are completely closed and staff working remotely.

Even when the mail is delivered there is no guarantee that the cards will end up in the hands of the right person. The potential for fraud is high, if they end up in the wrong hands. And of course, even if they just sit languishing in the mail room, if the existing card expires, the user will not be able to make additional purchases putting further stress on the supply chain.

Program administrators are urged to closely monitor the expiration dates on cards in their programs and have active communication with the card issuers to ensure cards are delivered as needed. This may mean asking the card issuer to mail cards directly to the homes of your employees. Some may not be comfortable with this.

In those rare instances where new cards were requested for employees who did not previously have cards, track their receipt closely. As with cards going to replace expiring cards, you will want to receive verification from the employee that they have both received their new card and activated it. In either case, if you are notified by the card issuer that a card has been activated but the employee has not received it, immediately cancel the card.

If your organization is one of the few that opens all the mail in the mailroom before it is distributed, this might be the time to review that practice. This is especially true, if you have any fraud related to this practice during the crisis.

Issue #2: Cards and Terminated Employees

While no one likes to talk about it, the fact is that employees do leave either of their own volition or by invitation. Often as the company scrambles to cover its operational bases making sure that former employee's tasks are covered, the T&E card or p-card given to the employee for company business is forgotten. And, let's face it, if the employee leaves with a bad taste in his or her mouth, leaving that card in his or her possession can be tempting fate.

Avoiding a Problem when an Employee Departs

Step 1. Mostly this issue will apply to those companies who provide their employees with cards. Employees should be instructed to turn in their cards as part of their exit process. In fact, if human resources conducts an exit interview or goes through a process where it gets back keys and employee ID cards, it can be instructed to also get back the any cards that may have been issued in the employees name.

Step 2. Immediately notify the card issuer and cancel the card. If you don't, a crafty employee can simply write down the card number, the expiration date and the CVC number. With that information they can go shopping online to their hearts content. Canceling the card is more important than getting the card back. If you can't get the card back immediately, due to the crisis or whatever, you will be covered if it is canceled with the bank. So, immediately, notify the financial institution.

Otherwise, in a small percentage of the cases, there will be a problem. This will occur when the employee uses the card for personal expenses. To a lesser extent the problem can occur if the employee was given a cash advance and never accounted for the funds, and/or perhaps never spent them on company business. (As cash advances continue to become less common, the cash-advance problem will become less and less of an issue.)

For starters, as part of the T&E as well as the employee manual, employees should be told that T&E cards need to be returned to the company when they depart. They also need to be informed that it is expected they will submit approved T&E reports for all company travel before they depart.

This is all fine and dandy when the parting is amicable. But occasionally it is not. Human resources should inform accounts payable or whoever is responsible for the T&E card program whenever an employee is fired. The cards of departing employees, whether fired or leaving of their own volition, should be terminated immediately.

Issue #3: Deceitful Use of Cards for Personal Gain

Cards (purchase, travel, fuel etc.), if used correctly, are a wonderful tool for organizations looking to run an efficient payment process. As part of the Lesser-Known Fraud Survey conducted early this year, respondents were asked about some low-dollar frauds. We were not expecting to see a high incidence of any of the frauds listed, so we were a bit startled at the level of certain petty frauds.

They are referred to as petty in that, for the most part, the dollar amounts involved are small. Each of the frauds involves significantly less than $10,000. In this piece, we take a look at some of the more common ways employees abuse company card programs as well as ways to prevent and detect those frauds.

Background

The number of ways employees defraud their employers through game playing with cards (both company and personal) is amazing. The accompanying chart on the next page summarizes the most common types of game-playing along with the percent of organizations where this has been found to occur. It also provides a summary chart of best practices that will prevent and/or detect the possible frauds.

Before we take an in-depth look at the best practices, let's be clear about one thing. The percentages shown indicate the proportion of organizations that have encountered the particular item, not the frequency of occurrence. So, for example, the 76.67% who indicated they have found personal non-Amazon orders charged with a company card does not mean that 76.67% of employees will play this game, just that it happened at least once (and probably more frequently than that) at 76.67% of all organizations participating in the survey.

Keep in mind that the numbers shown likely understate the problem, as respondents can only report frauds they have uncovered. And, if the fraud has gone undetected, then it can't be reported. Also, if the detailed meal receipt is not required, it is very difficult to determine if a gift card was added to a bill. So, the suspicion is that this type of fraud is a bit higher than reported.

As you review the list of items on the accompanying chart, some will note that we've included charitable contributions made at restaurants. You may be thinking, "that's not really fraud." And to a large extent you would be correct. However, and this is an important distinction, this is not the place for charitable donations to be made. If the employee wishes to donate to the charity in question, that is fine.

But by doing it as part of a meal, the fund will be charged to entertainment rather than charitable donations. What's more the charity in question might not advocate policies that are in line with the corporate policy. Think for example, about guns. No matter which side of that debate you are on, the charity in question might not hold the same position as the organization. Employees in all instances should be discouraged from making donations in the company's name without official authorization.

The Best Practices

As you look at the chart you will note that the best practices required to put a dent in this type of fraud are not esoteric, but something every company can do.

Best Practice #1: Start with a comprehensive detailed policy for both travel and use of p-card. This makes it crystal clear what is expected. What's more, many organizations include in their p-card policy a letter. This letter must be signed by any employee who is given a company card. In the letter the employee acknowledges he or she can be fired immediately, if they misuse the card. This makes it impossible for the employee committing the infraction to claim they didn't know. If they didn't read the policy, that is their problem not yours.

Best Practice #2: Require managers to review expense reports as well as charges put through by subordinates on company cards. This is probably the most overlooked control in virtually many, many organizations. AP Now surveys reveal that only about one-quarter of all managers regularly review the expenditures of their employees.

Most simply approve without reviewing what is on the report. This is unfortunate because the manager is in the best position to spot potential frauds and stop them. What's more, if the manager doesn't review eventually the employee comes to realize the manager isn't reviewing. In these instances, if they are so inclined, the employee will then take advantage of the situation and begin pushing the envelope.

Best Practice #3: Mandate use of company credit card. All the tricks that involve getting refunds simply disappear if the organization mandates the use of a company card and refuses to reimburse if the employee uses a personal card. Yet, almost half of all companies (47%) have a travel card for employees but make its use optional. For reasons that defy logic, even best practice organizations are willing to loosen controls in this regard.

Best Practice #4: Require detailed meal receipts. Of course, requiring the receipts only works as a control if someone actually reviews them. This doesn't mean that all the receipts must be reviewed in detail but it does mean they should be spot checked in detail. And of course, if the manager is reviewing everything, the accounts payable staff or the expense review staff doesn't have to worry about this issue.

The fact that organizations know about gift cards and charitable contributions means that employees are putting them through. Other questionable items that our readers have shared they found on detailed meal receipts include: takeout dinners (someone bringing an extra meal home for a spouse), a case of steaks from a fancy steakhouse, kiddie meals, and more. Detailed meal receipts are also a great way to document the absence of liquor for those with grants that prohibit such reimbursements.

Concluding Thoughts

The best practices discussed here are pretty basic and there is no good reason why organizations neglect to use them. Probably the most difficult change for most is to get managers to review expenditures by employees. Whether they are overworked, embarrassed to be seen nitpicking over expenses or simply believe their employees are honest is irrelevant. They need to do a much better job in this regard and if they do, lots of this petty game playing will simply disappear.

Yes, many employees prefer to use their personal cards for travel so they can accumulate loyalty points. But that is beside the point. When it creates extra work and/or loosens controls, priority must be given to running an efficient operation. Use of the practices discussed here will minimize, if not eliminate, many types of petty game playing.

Chapter 15: Expense Reporting Issues

While traditional expense reporting reimbursement requests have fallen dramatically, they have been replaced with reimbursement requests for expenses incurred while working at home. This creates a whole lot of new problems for those tasked with handling the compensation requests. Of particular complexity is the matter of Refunds (for conferences, seminars etc.) which is addressed in the next chapter.

Problem #1: Lack of Formal Policy

The sooner this issue is addressed the better. For one thing is certain. Every organization who sent their staffers home to work will find one or more employees have made purchases that defy reason and will expect their companies to reimburse them for those items. Already stories are starting to emerge about employees who have purchased expensive ergonomic chairs to use while working remotely.

While they certainly are within their rights to purchase whatever they wish, a few are expecting their companies to reimburse them for this expense and have submitted requests for this. Or, they have already put it on the corporate card. Thus, it is imperative that you update policy on this issue ASAP and include as much detail as possible.

By spelling out what is allowed and what is not, nothing is left to the employee's imagination. There are no decisions for them to make. Any time you have a problem with a reimbursement and discover it is due to poor or vague wording in the policy, update the policy and distribute the change to all affected parties.

Once the final policy has been created it should be shared with every impacted employee. This includes admins who frequently complete their bosses' reports and those who travel only occasionally. Many organizations post their policy on the organization's Intranet site while a few, most notably colleges and universities, post their policies on their Internet site.

The policy should be shared with every employee working remotely. Some of these employees might not have normally received a copy of the travel policy, since they don't travel. But this is different.

Problem #2: The Fairness Issue over What's Covered and What's Not

There has been some minor debate over what companies should be covering. Staffers have a difference of opinion. They are at both ends of the spectrum. Some take the stance that the employer should reimburse them for use of services they would have paid for anyway, while others are so thrilled to be working from home, they are happy to pay whatever incremental costs are involved.

What has become apparent is there is no one accepted practice. Here are some tactics currently being used:

- Some companies that provided commuter assistance are reallocating those funds to reimbursements for working from home expenses.

- Some companies are providing a small monthly stipend

- Some companies are providing a one-time flat fee of anywhere from $100-$250 per employee

- Some companies are taking the stance that any minor expenses the employee might encounter are more than offset by the saving in commuting expenses

Whatever approach is decided on, it should be agreed to as soon as possible and communicated to all employees. And then, it should be enforced uniformly. See next problem.

Problem #3: Ensuring Uniformity

Not only is 100% policy compliance desirable from a cost standpoint, allowing a select few individuals or departments to deviate from the policy can create unintentional HR issues. By allowing some employees to disregard the policy and spend above it you create a situation where it becomes impossible for the organization to terminate other employees for violating the same policy.

Should you try to terminate an employee for what is deemed a flagrant abuse, that employee could sue for discrimination if others were allowed to take the same liberties and not terminated. Talk to your HR manager about this and together approach management to implement a policy of zero tolerance for abuse of the policy. While this problem is no longer an issue for many organizations, a sizable minority continue to be plagued by it.

The problem here, as many have found with expense reimbursements, is to get management on board. Generally speaking, about 80% of all organizations report uniform enforcement. While that number is high, it means that there are problems with uniform enforcement at 20% of all organizations.

Problem #4: When the Employer Buys Lunch for Staff

The latest problem to rear its ugly head for a few companies involves reimbursing for meals and other perks while working. For most companies this is not an issue since they don't reimburse while working onsite, employees should not expect anything different when working remotely. However, a few organizations provide lots of goodies for employees during the working day. The most notable of these is Google, who is famed not only for the food they bring in but also other amenities.

The company recently drew headlines when it announced that its workers would not be allowed to expense food or fitness costs while working remotely during the COVID-19 crisis. They were so far as to say this was true even if there was cash left in an unused event or travel budget. While we imagine that some of the employee were not happy about this, Google did several things right here.

First, the created the policy and then announced it to employees before the crisis went on for too long. And then, they identified the loophole they suspected some might try to use as a workaround and closed it. And, they announced that as well.

Problem #5: Cancelation fees at hotels when employees didn't have time to cancel

Some hotels now have a policy of charging for one or more nights stay if the reservation is not canceled with 24 hours before the date of arrival. When it became apparent that organizations were going to quarantine with very little notice, travelers who were on the road spent many, many hours trying to get home. Some of them forgot to cancel their hotel reservations. Likewise, some events were canceled with only a few weeks' notice and attendees may have forgotten they'd made a hotel reservation.

How are hotels reacting? Some, but definitely not all, are charging the no-show fee for those who forgot to cancel. Your mission is to first identify these charges and then have the employee in question try and negotiate with the hotel. You can call upon their goodwill or your past activity your whole organization has had with them.

Keep in mind though, that some of the hotels you think are part of a chain, may actually be a franchise and not care about your activity with the rest of the chain.

Problem #6: Fraud

Cards (purchase, travel, fuel etc.), if used correctly, are a wonderful tool for organizations looking to run an efficient payment process. As part of the Lesser-Known Fraud Survey conducted early this year, respondents were asked about some low-dollar frauds. We were not expecting to see a high incidence of any of the frauds listed, so we were a bit startled at the level of certain petty frauds. They are referred to as petty in that, for the most part, the dollar amounts involved are small. Each of the frauds involves significantly less than $10,000. In this piece, we take a look at some of the more common ways employees abuse company card programs as well as ways to prevent and detect those frauds.

The number of ways employees defraud their employers through game playing with cards (both company and personal) is amazing. The accompanying chart on the next page summarizes the most common types of game-playing along with the percent of organizations where this has been found to occur. It also provides a summary chart of best practices that will prevent and/or detect the possible frauds.

Let's be clear about one thing. The percentages shown indicate the proportion of organizations that have encountered the particular item, not the frequency of occurrence. So, for example, the 76.67% who indicated they have found personal non-Amazon orders charged with a company card does not mean that 76.67% of employees will play this game, just that it happened at least once (and probably more frequently than that) at 76.67% of all organizations participating in the survey.

Keep in mind that the numbers shown likely understate the problem, as respondents can only report frauds they have uncovered. And, if the fraud has gone undetected, then it can't be reported. Also, if the detailed meal receipt is not required, it is very difficult to determine if a gift card was added to a bill. So, the suspicion is that this type of fraud is a bit higher than reported.

As you review the list of items on the accompanying chart, some will note that we've included charitable contributions made at restaurants. You may be thinking, "that's not really fraud." And to a large extent you would be correct. However, and this is an important distinction, this is not the place for charitable donations to be made. If the employee wishes to donate to the charity in question, that is fine.

But by doing it as part of a meal, the fund will be charged to entertainment rather than charitable donations. What's more the charity in question might not advocate policies that are in line with the corporate policy. Think for example, about guns. No matter which side of that debate you are on, the charity in question might not hold the same position as the organization. Employees in all instances should be discouraged from making donations in the company's name without official authorization.

Tips for Preventing Expense Reporting Fraud

Here is a course of action any organization can follow to ensure the lowest level of Expense Reporting fraud possible. While you can never completely eliminate fraud attempts, you can make is so difficult that the crooks take their trade elsewhere.

Step one. Have a detailed written policy, periodically updated and available to all. This way no one can say, "I didn't know that."

Step two. Make sure the policy enforced uniformly, no exceptions. In an *AP Now* survey, 80% of the respondents indicated the T&E policy was enforced uniformly in their organizations. Once exceptions are made, everyone feels entitled to take advantage.

Step three. Spot check reports making sure to do an in-depth review of those reports reviewed. Give processors the authority to question anything that looks suspicious. When spot-checking select:

- Some reports at random;

- All reports over a certain dollar level considered high for your organization;

- All reports of known rogue spenders; and

- All high-level executives, if that is your policy.

Step four. Each year select a certain number of traveling employees for a 14-month review. This should include a selection as above. Review each employee's reports for the 14 months together. Sometimes fraud that does not appear when reviewing reports singly jumps out when looked at together. For example, receipts in numerical order might not be noticed when reviewing individually.

Step five. Have a zero-tolerance policy. This should be spelled out clearly in the beginning of the policy, ideally in a letter signed by a high-level executive.

Step six. Make the approving manager both professionally and financially responsible for any report he/she approves. This helps put an end to the practice of approving reports without looking at what is on them.

Step seven. Require two approving signatures on all reports over a certain level. The fact that the report will have a second review often puts pressure on the first approver to review a little more carefully.

Expense reporting fraud should never have been tolerated. Incorporate the program detailed above and you will be one step closer to eliminating it from the landscape at your organization.

Chapter 16: The New Nightmare: Tracking and Handling Refunds (Conventions etc.)

Refunds for cancelled events many have occurred very occasionally in the past, since COVID-19 and quarantine, it has become a huge issue. Ensuring that all refunds from canceled conferences, seminars, prepaid hotel stays etc. are returned. This means not only getting the funds back from the event arranger. It also means making sure to retrieve the refund from any employees who may have used their personal card to pay for the event. This will mean extra work at a time when employees will be stretched thin with other tasks. Perhaps this will change some executives' minds on this less-than-ideal practice. But I'm getting ahead of the story. In this chapter we'll look at practices related to:

- The Event: Canceled or rescheduled

- The Cancelled Event: Refund or credit for future event

- The related travel expenses: Airlines, hotels, etc.

- When the expense was put on a personal card and reimbursed

Overview

In AP Now's 2018 survey on Lesser-Known Frauds, 17% of the survey participants reported having a problem with employees canceling flights and "forgetting" to return the refund to the company. Additionally, 8% reported cancelled events with the employee not remembering to return the refund to their organization. And, these figures only reflect instances where the deception was uncovered. Likely, they are higher.

In the aftermath of the COVID-19 crisis, canceled or postponed events are likely to be a huge problem for program managers for several reasons:

- *The Postponement*: Some events weren't cancelled but merely postponed. This will create a tracking nightmare for those responsible.

- *The Options*: In some cases when an event was canceled, employees were given the choice of either getting a refund or moving the registration to the next year's event.

- *The Problem Date*: In some cases, the event was canceled, it was merely postponed for several months. The new date may or may not work for the employee.

- *The Forgetful Employee*: When an employee is allowed to use personal cards instead of a company card, this problem is exacerbated, especially since the card program manager often is not even aware of the booking. As the above statistics indicate, employees either forget or knowingly mislead their organizations when it comes to returning refunds.

- *The Changed Travel Policy*: In some cases, where events were postponed or registrations rolled to next year's events, the organization's travel policy may change. The new registration may be at odds with the policy.

- *The Terminated Employee*: In some cases, employees who receive the refund will have been terminated due to overall staff reductions.

- *The Changed Price*: If this isn't enough, a few hosting organizations are changing the price when they take the event online. Some are reducing it, others are allowing more than one attendee for the one price and a few other have actually raised the price.

- *The Ancillary Reservations*: For many, there were also hotel reservations and airline reservations that had to be dealt with.

- *Cancelation Fees*: Some events were canceled just as the crisis broke. Other employees were traveling and had to abruptly turn around and come home. Many caught in that situation forgot to cancel hotel reservations and some of those hotels have charged mandatory cancelation fees. These often amount to one or two nights stay in the hotel.

We'll look at each of these in a little more detail but before we do, let's discuss the tracking nightmare this is creating for professionals responsible for administering expense reimbursements.

Tracking

This whole issue is made a lot easier to handle if the organization simply gets a refund for the event and then rebooks, if and when the new session takes place, assuming the date works and the travel policy hasn't changed. However, most mired in the tracking of this mess are doing so after the fact. Each employee made their own decision, often encouraged by the hosting organization to move the registration to the next year or new date.

Since this is largely a matter of cleaning up after the fact, there's no time to set policy. It will be a monumental tracking and monitoring task. It already looks like some events that were rescheduled will have to reschedule a second time or make other arrangements.

Begin by searching your expense reimbursements to identify all events that have been paid for starting with events in March 2020. Once you have your Master List, you can track using that. Watch expense reports coming in for the next few months to see if any additional events have been scheduled.

The Postponed Event

In this case, the hosting organization simply moved the date of the event, in the hopes that the crisis would pass quickly. When this happened, attendees could either get a refund or move to the new event. They were encouraged to move to the new date. In fact, in some cases, they were just moved. Some sponsors readily gave attendance fees back and others made it more difficult.

Unfortunately, the crisis hit just before the start of spring conference season, so this is likely to be an issue for most companies. Someone, probably someone who works on expense reports, should be put in charge of the effort to track refunds and rescheduled events. If is important that you follow-up close to the reschedule dates to find out what happened and get a refund if it is warranted.

This is apt to be a long-term project, given that some events were rescheduled for a year out.

When There Were Options

As mentioned earlier, some events gave attendees the choice of a refund or a registration at next year's event. While it would have been easier if the employee simply took the refund, few companies had a policy on this matter as we went into the crisis.

So, if your employee took the registration for next year, mark it down for follow up in a year. And, if your employee went for the refund, make sure the money comes back to the organization and is accounted for in the correct manner.

The Problem Date

If the event was rescheduled, and the reschedule date does not work for the employee, a refund is in order. Some hosting organizations may try and push back. But stand your ground. They did not deliver the product as promised so you're entitled to a refund.

If things get really sticky, contact your credit card company. Only a very few organizations will give you a hard time about this. Most are being quite accommodating.

The Forgetful Employee

In almost 50% of all organizations, management allows the weak practice of permitting employees use personal credit cards for company business travel expenses. In the case of refund for an event that the company paid for, the refund will end up on the employees' personal cards. The employees should immediately turn that refunds over to the company.

But guess what? A few employees will forget to return the refund to the company. To be fair, some honestly will forget. But others knowingly hold onto that refund. Therefore, as part of your tracking, you will need to follow up, possibly several times, with these employees. This is just one I'll be extreme, example of why employees should not be using their own credit cards for company business.

The Updated Travel Policy

Without a doubt, more than a few organizations will experience financial difficulty over the next year or two. This is as a result of COVID-19. Typically, when an organization experiences financial difficulty, one of the things that gets cut is travel and education, especially conferences and seminars.

So, if you have an event that was canceled and the registration moved to the next year, and your company changes its travel policy, you will need to deal with the employee over airfare hotel and other ancillary expenses. If the company declines to reimburse the employee for them, and the employee does not choose to pay them himself, you could lose the conference registration.

It is recommended that you try and get the refund at that point, but clearly it will be a little tricky.

The Terminated Employee

When a conference or seminar refund is given it is typically refunded to the cord that was used initially for the transaction. If it was a personal card then the refund goes on the personal card. If you have this situation when an employee, either through no fault of their own or through their own fault, is terminated you now are in the on enviable position of trying to get that employee to turn the refund back over to the company.

While you should definitely make an attempt to get that money back from the employee there's a chance you8 won't be able to. This is just one more example of why putting company charges on personal cards is a bad idea.

They Change the Price

You can't make this stuff up. In some cases when event moves online, the prices changed. There have been examples of the conference going to a zero cost and the hosting organization refunding all the fees. That has evolved into situations where the event is held online and a different fee is charged. In some cases the fees were lowered and the difference is refunded to the card where the transaction was originally charged. In other cases, the registrants were told that for the same fee they can now bring several more people.

And in a few cases the price of the conference has been increased. There are a variety of reasons why the conference host might increase the price. They might feel that the company is not spending money on hotel and airfare and therefore can afford to spend more money on the event. Or more likely, they feel that the company will probably share the links with more than one attendee (not during the live event but afterwards).

Whatever the reason it doesn't matter. The fees are changed this creates an additional tracking dilemma for the company.

Another issue if they've raised the price, the new price may be outside the guidelines of what the organization is willing to pay for a conference so additional tracking issues will arise.

Ancillary Reservations

In addition to a conference or seminar, the employee probably made reservations for a hotel and airline. In some cases, the hotel might have been pre-paid or might have required deposit of one or two nights. With the airlines if the reservation was made, clearly they are that had to be paid for.

So, in addition to tracking the conference or the seminar refunds, make sure all refunds are received, and you also need to follow up on the hotel and the airlines. There have been reports of a few service providers (airlines and hotels) who have been reluctant to give the money back although most of been quite good about it. In some case, with the airlines, employees may have accepted a credit rather than the refund. So, yes, yet another tracking challenge.

Cancellation Fees

Some hotels require you cancel within 24 or 48 hours before your reservation if you are not going to come. With all the hoop dee dah that went on when this crisis first emerged a few employees forgot to cancel hotel reservations.

Unfortunately, not all hotels understood and forgave those cancellation fees. Some did charge them. If one of your employees was charged, you can prevail upon the hotels good nature to see if you can get it refunded. But some won't give it back. It's probably not a huge amount of money so you might not want to spend too much time on it. But be aware that this is out there

Chapter 17: Going Paperless

Of course, the subject of going paperless in the accounts payable function has been discussed in professional circles for many years. However, progress, especially on the payment front, has not been as robust as many would like. The COVID-19 crisis in the spring of 2020 highlighted many of the difficulties in a paper-based process. In this chapter we take a look at the overall philosophy and tactics that can be used by those that are just getting started. There are also a few tips for those looking to amp of their efforts in programs that were started but need to gain some momentum. In this section we look at:

- Getting Started

- Invoices via e-Mail

- Reducing the Number of Paper Checks Issued

- Other Tactics for Those Looking to Go Paperless without Spending a Cent

- Paperless 1099s

Getting Started when Going Paperless: Five Baby Steps.

While it is unlikely that we'll see an accounts payable office that is 100% free of paper anytime soon, the profession is making great strides towards that goal. But, progress has been uneven, with larger companies making more progress in the battle to get rid of some of the paper. AP Now has heard from a number of its readers, primarily at mid-size companies, that they'd like to get started eliminating the paper from their operations, but they don't know where to start.

What follows is a look at five simple approaches any organization can take to win that first clash against the paper.

Step 1: Accept/encourage e-mailed invoices. Most, if not all readers, are probably already receiving some invoices through e-mail. This eliminates mail time thus making it easier to earn early payment discounts and quickly identify discrepant invoices that need special attention. It also helps avoid potential postal problems. Once the staff becomes comfortable and proficient handling e-mailed invoices, consider encouraging a broader base of vendors to submit by e-mail. While this is not complete invoice automation, it is a good step in the right direction. Ideally, you should set up a separate e-mail address to receive invoices and nothing else.

Step 2: Encourage e-payments by offering to e-mail remittance information. One of the biggest obstacles for some vendors when it comes to accepting electronic payments is the absence of the remittance information needed to apply the cash.

Step 3: Look into one of the third-party automated travel and expense reporting systems available on a pay-as-you-go basis. This is a huge step forward, even if you are currently using an Excel spreadsheet that is e-mailed for approvals and processing. Implementation is fairly simple and you'll get 100% policy checking, if you choose.

Step 4: Improve the statement audit process by requesting vendors e-mail their statements to you. While the whole statement audit process can be outsourced, if you choose to handle it in-house, request that vendors send statements (with all information) electronically. If you can get them to provide the information in an Excel spreadsheet instead of PDF files, even better.

Step 5: Look into providing electronic Form 1099s instead of mailing paper ones in January. (See the article on page x for additional information). This is one great way to get the paper out of your office while making an odious task a little more palpable.

Some Caveats

To get the most out of these approaches, keep in mind the following:

1) Don't print out information that was e-mailed to you. Make sure your staff is aware of this caveat. Invoices that were e-mailed can be forwarded to the appropriate party for approval.

2) Start where you are most comfortable. It's not imperative that the first paperless move you make is at the top of the list. Do what is likely to be the least troublesome for your group to implement.

3) Start slowly and iron out any unexpected snafus that appear along the way. Don't try and convert an entire accounts payable process in one fell swoop. Of course, the expense reporting and electronic 1099s will have to be done all at one time, once you've *adequately* tested the process. However, when it comes to the issues of accepting invoices electronically and making electronic payments, start small with a group of trusted partners. Once you've made sure the process works, you can roll it out to a larger group.

4) Expect staff resistance when it comes to implementing change. Regardless of how much easier their jobs will be after the change, there is almost always a group who prefer things the old way. By anticipating this conflict, you'll be able to address it adequately and move the project forward on schedule.

5) Be aware that some vendors who e-mail invoices will also send paper ones to ensure you receive at least one copy. Most who do this are not trying to trick you into making a duplicate payment, although a few might be. Make sure your duplicate payment checking routines are all in place to weed out possible duplicates.

Concluding Thoughts

Automation and an almost paperless accounts payable function are facts of life. Where each organization stands on the paper spectrum depends in some part on the actions taken by the manager of the department. To move away from the 100% paper portion of the spectrum, try the tactics suggested above. In all likelihood, once you get started, you'll find yourself looking for ways to expand these strategies and look for new ways to banish more paper from your accounts payable function.

Making the Most of No-Cost Technology: A Policy for Vendors Submitting Invoices via e-Mail for Payment.

No longer does an organization have to spend a small fortune to gain the benefits of technology and/or to go paperless. In fact, AP Now has found a number of organizations who are using no-cost technology to streamline their accounts payable operations, in unique ways. What follows is an amalgamation of the process used in several organizations to receive e-mail.

The Basic Philosophy

The organizations who take this approach have decided they are fed up with all the paper and want to eliminate as much of it as possible. Yet, they are not ready to sign up for an automated invoice processing service offered by third-party providers.

They have decided to encourage suppliers to send invoices via e-mail. Many of the companies that go down this road are already receiving some (most) of their invoices in this manner. Suppliers are asked to convert their invoices to a PDF and then e-mail them in.

Some offer a fax alternative for those vendors who don't seem to be able to create a PDF of their invoices. Of course, what these suppliers don't realize is that the company has married its fax with an e-fax service, so they are not receiving the paper, but an e-mail of the fax.

The Invoice by E-mail Only Policy

By getting all invoices electronically, paper invoices no longer are a factor. Here's several sample policies you can use:

1. All vendors are encouraged to submit their invoices by e-mail.

2. All vendors are required to submit their invoices by e-mail.

3. All vendors are required to submit their invoices by e-mail or fax.

Which approach you decide to take, will depend on your philosophy and your tolerance for the headache dealing with paper invoices.

When receiving invoices by e-mail, a separate address should be set up for this purpose. Do not use an employee's e-mail for this purpose. It creates too many problems when the employee is out unexpectedly or on vacation. It also increases the chance of getting lost. Also, several people should have access to this e-mail account, so there is adequate backup when the primary employee is absent. Some organizations divide the responsibility for checking the invoice e-mail account between several employees.

Best Practices for E-mailed Invoices

Suppliers should be provided with some guidelines for submitting invoices by e-mail. Here are a few best practices regarding that issue:

1. The subject line should include a standard statement such as Invoice Attached and the PO number.

2. Invoices should be sent to the e-mail address and nowhere else. There is no need to send copies to other parties. This just increases the chances of them being processed and possibly paid twice.

3. Each invoice should be in a separate PDF.

4. If there is backup documentation, that may be included in the same PDF file, although the invoice must be the first page.

5. Each invoice should be sent in a separate e-mail.

6. There is no need to include a cover memo or note with the invoice. The first page of the PDF file should be the invoice itself.

7. The PDF should be sent as an attachment. Invoice information should not be pasted into the body of the e-mail message.

8. Statements and other correspondence should not be sent to the e-mail address set up for the receipt of invoices.

Other Invoice Policies

Regardless of the approach taken, there are some basics that should be incorporated into the invoice receipt policy. These should be shared with vendors. They include:

1. All invoices must include a PO number or the name of the purchaser

2. All invoices should be centrally received and the e-mail address and/or fax number and/or postal address provided to the vendor

Would accepting invoices only by e-mail make your accounts payable operation run a little bit smoother? If so, you might want to investigate adopting such a policy.

Reducing the Number of Paper Checks Issued

Paper checks are a necessary evil. They are probably the most inefficient way a company can pay its bills, yet they are the way most organizations handle their invoices. What follows is a quick look at five ways any group can reduce the number of paper checks it issues followed by an explanation of three processes that will reduce the number of paper checks but are not recommended as the create more problems than they solve.

Try These

1) P-cards. Start a p-card program for use on small dollar invoices. If you already have a program, look to see what else can be included in the program, further reducing the number of paper checks.

2) T & E reimbursements. Where appropriate, have employees pay for something under the T&E umbrella and then submit for reimbursement along with their T&E. Of course, for this to work, proper controls must be in place to ensure the item isn't paid for twice.

3) A credit card for AP. If you don't have a p-card program consider getting one card for accounts payable and using that card to pay any invoice that can be paid using a credit card. This approach is especially successful for those organizations with lots of subscriptions. Just about every publisher takes credit cards. If your organization does have a p-card program, make sure one is issued to someone in accounts payable to pay those miscellaneous invoices that can be paid with a credit card.

4) For those vendors who send many low-dollar invoices, consider going to a summary billing approach or paying from statements, if you can implement the proper controls to ensure no invoice will get paid, this is a real winner.

5) Convert as many vendors to ACH as possible. We've saved the best for last. When it comes to reducing the number of paper checks being produced, this is the "killer app."

What Not to Do

1) Refuse to pay invoices under a certain dollar amount. A few organizations have a minimum dollar amount for checks. While this may seem like a great way to reduce the number of checks written, it can backfire. While you can usually find a way to avoid issuing a check for five dollars, there may be those rare occasions when you can't. We know of one organization that stopped doing business with a vendor who took this approach.

2) Rely on a petty cash box. Yes, paper checks are an expensive inefficient way to pay invoices, but a petty cash box is a worse way to handle your obligations. As regular readers of this publication are aware, AP Now strongly advocates for the complete elimination of petty cash boxes.

3) Hold payments until you accumulate a certain dollar threshold and then issue a check for the total. While this may seem to make sense on one level, you could end up carrying certain balances for a very long time.

As you can see, there are a number of approaches that can be used to reduce the number of paper checks issued. Just make sure you avoid the last three. They'll create other problems much worse than paper checks. And you don't want to take one step forward and then two backwards, which is exactly what you'd with these three tactics.

Strategies to Facilitate the Process of Eliminating Paper Checks

Many of those organizations that rely heavily on paper checks learned the hard way, during the COVID-19 crisis, that they are not necessarily the most efficient payment mechanism.

While you might find that news mildly interesting, what you are probably more interested in is just how they managed to make those changes. A number of respondents to a recent AP Now survey shared their strategies for making the shift away from paper checks. But before we discuss the strategies you can use, we thought you'd be interested in one of the other findings.

The Paper Check Findings

There was a dichotomy between those who fall under the heading of heavy check users and those who are considered low check users. Here's how each of those groups are defined:

- Low check users are those who make less than half of their B2B payments using paper checks. 28% of the respondents fell into this category.

- Heavy check users are those who make more than 75% of their B2B payments using paper checks. Alas, 51% of the respondents fell into this category.

There is a big divide in the goals each of these groups has to further reduce the number of paper checks they issue. While 100% of the low check users want to further reduce the number of paper checks they issue, only 45% of the heavy check users have the same goal. What's more, another 45% of the heavy check users are satisfied with the status quo while 86% of the low check users had formal plans in place to further reduce their reliance on paper checks. Of course, this was before the crisis.

Theoretically, if these groups follow through with their plans, we could end up with some companies issuing virtually no paper checks while others continue for years to wallow in their paper check muddle.

Approaches to Reduce the Number of Paper Checks

The list below includes some of the best approaches for diminishing the number of paper checks. Before you start, we warn you that you might find some of them quite aggressive. That being said, they appear to be working.

The Gentle Approach

- Attach an EFT form to the request for a W-9 whenever contacting vendors for the TIN information.

- Have AP team members include EFT information in their signature. Outgoing message from your main AP e-mailbox should also include ACH signup information. For both of these, tout the benefits of ACH, as one respondent indicates: It's Green, It's Faster, And It's Secure.

- Greater use of virtual and ghost cards will impact the number of paper checks in a positive way.

- Send out notes with every check payment explaining how the vendor can change to electronic payments. Make it easy for them.

The Encouraging Middle of the Road Approach

- Work with Purchasing to move vendors to Electronic payments and supply chain financing at the same time.

- Directly ask that existing vendors begin accepting EFT. Sometimes, all it takes is a simple request, but if you don't ask, they won't volunteer.

- Reach out to frequently paid vendors requesting they use EFT. Include your signup form if your request is being made by mail.

- Print checks once per week while making ACH payments every day. When a vendor requests a Rush payment, direct them to ACH – unless they wish to wait until the next check run.

- Promote ACH as your preferred payment method, and default with new suppliers. Make new suppliers ask for check payment, if they wish to be paid that way. When they ask, point out the benefits of ACH.

- Review the number of check vendors on a monthly basis, and attempt to arrange for them to receive ACH or card payments. If you start with the vendors who are receiving the highest volume of checks, you'll get a better return for your efforts.

- Have new Vendors sign up on your vendor portal and provide a link to join paymode for ACH payments. Make this the recommended payment vehicle when they complete the vendor profile.

- Look at high transaction check vendors and reach out to get them to sign up for electronic payments.

- Email or mail ACH Authorization forms to vendors who are not yet set up to receive electronic payments

- Work with Product/sales to initiate ACH up front with the product offers, making it part of the new vendor process. If sales will sell it as a benefit, some will sign on.

- Require direct deposit for all employee T & E reimbursements

- Include in the original vendor setup calls that you prefer to pay with a credit card or ACH. Make it easy for them to give you the information you need to make their payments electronically.

The Aggressive Approach

- Mandated EFT payments for all new suppliers and employees, if the law allows. In many states, you cannot mandate direct deposit of payroll.

- In order to do business with you, vendors must accept ACH starting 2016. You might want to ensure management and purchasing are on board with this before taking this approach.

- Reduce check payments from twice a month to once a month.

- Call your vendors and tell (don't ask) them you need the EFT information because you are transitioning away from paper checks.

- Reduce the number of check runs to force the issue.

- Set a policy of not setting up new vendors without first obtaining bank information for ACH payments.

Other Tactics for Those Looking to Go Paperless without Spending a Cent

If you are like most people affiliated with the accounts payable function, you'd probably do almost anything to get rid of the mountains of paper. If you are lucky, you work for a company that actually has budget to do just that *and* has spent it on that process. Alas, many of the rest of us can only dream of such an existence. But this does not have to be. Lack of budget does not mean you have to completely forgo the benefits of an electronic accounts payable department. Let's take a look at seven strategies any organization can use to get rid of some of the paper—and they don't cost a red cent.

1) Start accepting invoices electronically. Typically, e-mailed invoices arrive in the form of a PDF attachment. If you print the attachment, you're not getting rid of much paper. So, figure out how you want to store these documents in a centralized location. Some retraining of processors might also be called for as they learn how to deal with an electronic document instead of a paper one.

2) Have faxed invoices sent to an e-fax facility. This will automatically convert faxes to e-mails and you'll never have to deal with the paper. Once you have this in placed, your so-called faxed invoices can be treated exactly like e-mailed invoices.

3) Make payments to vendors electronically. This will help get rid of those awful paper checks. And, not only will you get rid of some of the paper, electronic payments are cheaper than paper checks.

4) Send remittance advices to vendors for e-payments via e-mail. This simple step will make a huge difference in whether or not some vendors accept payments electronically. By providing this information directly to the person handling cash applications, the problems many vendors have with electronic payments disappear. And, again, there's no paper.

5) Send an e-mail with explanations of short payments to vendors, if information doesn't fit on remittance advice. The beauty of this approach is by taking the initiative you not only improve vendor relationships; you also reduce the number of calls coming into accounts payable.

6) Automate your expense reporting process even if it's only e-mailing an Excel version of your expense reports for approval and then for reimbursement. Of course, if using Excel remember to lock the formulas to prevent employees from trying to play games with reimbursement requests.

7) Make electronic payments (ACH) mandatory for all expense reimbursements. While many states still will not allow you to mandate electronic payments for payroll, you can do so for expense reimbursements.

As you can see, none of the strategies proposed are difficult or require budget. They may necessitate a change in process, but that is easily managed. And once you've made these changes, don't forget to update your policy and procedures manual as well as train all affected employees.

Paperless 1099s

With the relentless drive to banish paper from the accounts payable departments, every single function is being analyzed to see what can be done to get on the electronic wagon. This is even true of those dreaded 1099s. IRS Revenue Procedure 2012-38 details the requirements for withholding agents looking to provide electronic Forms 1099 MISC.

The Requirements

Specifically, the withholding agent must:

- Obtain affirmative client consent to receiving the Form 1099 MISC electronically which is withdrawn prior to the statement being furnished.

    a. Consent must be made electronically in a way that shows that client can access the statement in the electronic format.

- Notify the recipient of any hardware or software changes that may impact their ability to obtain the statement prior to furnishing the statement.

    a. Must obtain new consent to receive the statement electronically after the new hardware or software is put into service.

- Provide the recipient a statement with the following statements prominently displayed prior to providing the statement electronically:

1. A paper copy will be provided if recipient does not consent to receive the statement electronically

2. Scope and duration of consent

3. How to obtain a paper copy after giving consent

4. How to withdraw the consent

5. Notice of termination

6. How to update the recipient's information

7. Description of the hardware and software required to access, print and retain a statement, and a date the statement will no longer be available on the website.

- Post, on or before the due date, the applicable statement on a website that will be accessible to the recipient through October 15 of that year.

- Inform the recipient, electronically or by mail, of the posting and how to access and print the statement.

What This Means for Most Organizations

Without a doubt, it is costly to produce and mail those paper forms, regardless of whether you do it yourself or outsource the function. The electronic format reduces the cost and makes it easier to replace lost forms.

Given the aggravation and cost of printing and mailing electronic forms, it's certainly an attractive option. If you have not already started to make arrangements to provide your Form 1099s in an electronic format, it's only a matter of time before you will. Familiarize yourself with the requirements so when management comes with its request to go electronic, you will be ready.

Chapter 18: Fraud During A Crisis

Without a doubt, crooks look to take advantage of any weakness they perceive in an organization. The target can be either financial or data. Needless to say, the COVID-19 crisis has provided these criminals a golden opportunity – and they are looking to make hay while the sun shines, so to speak.

In this section, we'll take a look at some of the newer frauds and how you can protect your organization. But have no doubt, there will be additional frauds. We start with a short section on a best practice that will provide a good amount (but of course, not complete) protection. In this section we'll investigate the following:

- The Silver Bullet

- Business Email Compromise Fraud

- Vendor Impersonation Fraud

- Some Newer Frauds

- Other Payment Frauds and How They Can Be Prevented

- Hiding Places: Looking for Fraud in All the Right Places

The Silver Fraud Prevention Bullet

I believe that education is the silver bullet when it comes to many social issues. So, I was a little taken back when I realized that the same can be said for payment fraud. But the more I thought about it and looked at the various talks I give related to payment fraud, the clearer it became.

Case in Point: There have been a number of municipalities defrauded by the common business email compromise scam. As many of our members and readers are aware, schemers research companies already working with their targets thoroughly in order to spoof a company email and assume the identity of a trusted individual within a company. They then request a wire fraud transfer using dollar amounts in line with business transactions that make sense to the municipality. According to the FBI, the Town of Farmington lost $2 million this way. Several other towns and at least one community college lost money this way.

How Education Would Have Helped: By simply knowing these frauds were going on, employees might have been able to recognize a fraudulent request when they received one. They also would have known not to jump just because the email looked like it came from a high-level executive.

Takeaway: It is no longer adequate to just take steps that worked in the past to protect your organization against all the different types of fraud that exist and are being created constantly. It is critical that everyone keep up.

Business Email Compromise Fraud

According to the United States' Federal Bureau of Investigation (FBI), business email compromise (BEC) is a scam frequently carried out when a subject compromises legitimate business email accounts through social engineering or computer intrusion techniques to conduct unauthorized transfers of funds. Global BEC losses exceeded USD $12B in 2018. Over 95% of AP Now's readers report having been targeted with this type of fraud.

Background

The scammers, believed to be members of organized crime groups from Africa, Eastern Europe, and the Middle East, primarily target businesses that work with foreign suppliers or regularly perform wire transfer payments. The scam succeeds by compromising legitimate business e-mail accounts through social engineering or computer intrusion techniques.

Businesses of all sizes are targeted, and the fraud is proliferating. No one is exempt.

Do not rest easy because your business doesn't have foreign suppliers. Others are emulating the fraud. AP Now has heard several reports from domestic organizations and local not-for-profits where C-level executives' email accounts were compromised and used in a similar manner.

The Savvy Fraudster

If you are wondering how it is possible that so many companies fell for this fraud, the answer is simple. The folks involved with committing this fraud are smart and they do their homework. When they target a company they use language specific to that organization and only ask for dollar amounts that will not raise a red flag. Thus on the face of it, the request does not look odd.

Similar to an ACH corporate account takeover fraud, the crooks often employ malware to gain access to company networks. They then infiltrate legitimate e-mail threads sometimes impersonating a vendor and sometimes the customer. They understand the billing practices of the supplier. They also know how the invoice process works. They craft their fraud to avoid raising suspicions of the employee involved when a fraudulent wire transfer is requested.

They also have used this type of an approach to obtain confidential information they are not entitled to. So, while money is definitely their primary goal, it is not the only area to be concerned about.

Protecting Your Organization

This is a serious threat and one every organization must safeguard itself against. What follows is a five-step plan that will help your organization defend itself against this insidious fraud.

Step 1: Make sure everyone affected knows about the fraud and what to expect. This means alerting the staff but it also means alerting senior management. Why? Because as you will see in Step 2, they need to not only know what is going on, but also to expect that junior staffers will sometimes question their instructions. If you are to prevent a BEC fraud, then staffers will end up questioning legitimate transactions as well as those that are truly fraudulent.

Step 2: Employees will need to start verifying any request they receive that is outside the normal channels. This includes Rush wire instructions from a CEO or CFO as well as change of bank account instructions from vendors. This verification cannot be done by simply replying to an email with the original instructions. For if they were sent by a crook, they will most certainly be verified if you go back to them and ask for confirmation using the original email address.

Step 3: Beef up the contact information in the master vendor file. That way, when a request for change of bank account for payment comes in, you can contact the vendor using contact information you have on hand. This data should be collected when the vendor is first set up in the master vendor file.

Step 4: Regularly update the contact information in the master vendor file. While getting it when the vendor is first step up is a great first step, people change jobs frequently and the information you have on hand will quickly become outdated. You can expect at least half of it to be inaccurate after five years. So, at least once a year, ping all your vendors for contact information updates.

Step 5: Learn how to use the forward key instead of the reply key when responding to messages. When you hit forward and start typing the email address in of the respondent, the computer will auto-fill in the address. This will mean you are responding to your real contact and not someone impersonating that person. While this sounds easy enough to do, it is incredibly difficult to remember in practice. We invite all our readers to try.

The accompanying table contains additional steps you can take to protect your organization.

What to Do if You've Been Scammed

If indeed you do find out that you've been scammed, call your bank immediately. They may be able to get some or all of your money back. Do not wait. Time is of the essence if you want to have a recovery. Also, report the theft to the FBI, filing a complaint with the IC3.

Uncovering BEC Fraud

In our recent Fraud survey, we asked about Business Email Compromise Fraud. Many of our members have been hit by attempts of this type. They shared with us how they uncovered these fraudulent requests and their responses are instructive. Here are some of the more insightful responses.

- The person responsible for completing the bank transfer checked with the person, prior to initiating any transfer, to verify validity of request.

- Called the CEO to verify

- The AP staff is trained on what to look for - ie scroll over the email address to be sure it's internal.

- Recognized that the request was unusual and did not follow our standard procedures

- I never receive these types of requests from our CEO and the email address was not correct.

- Thanks to information from AP sources such as AP Now I was aware of the fraud.

- Staff were suspicious.

- The email address was clearly not the correct address for our CEO.

- Crazy requests didn't make sense

- Awareness that we don't issue checks upon just an email from the CEO.

- AP recognized the request as fraud.

- Our CEO would follow the processes in place for a rush payment - she wouldn't request it through email. We would call her to verify that she made the request.

- The person's name that they compromised wouldn't request or authorize wires. And the email address (long form) looked off

- Email address was noted as incorrect.

- The email address and signature in the request were not standard. The COO and CFO were not copied on the email.

- The email request didn't follow our processes therefore it was caught right away.

- The email was signed using the CEO formal name and not the name he prefers.

- Although the email showed the CEO it was a mass email thru another server.

- Our IT department circulated a fraud notice when the first email was discovered

- The fraudster used the name of an employee who was no longer with the company. The AP clerk realized that the request was a fraud.

- We routinely review the actual email sender's address.

- E-mail supposedly from Chairman - She is not in same city and would never request a new vendor be set up, or for an ACH or wire payment to be made

- IT department is incorporating additional training tools to inform staff of fraudulent examples and what not to do when reviewing emails.

- The type of fraud was discussed among finance team. Agreed that email from one of our principals for funds transfer was never the proper protocol. Email was sent to me, the controller, and I advised principals of this attempt.

- Checked email address of sender since CEO would not be requesting the wire, then verified with CEO.

- The CEO doesn't normally make wire requests and the email just seemed odd so it was verified with a phone call to the CEO.

- I received an email from a former employee who is now a VP with another company and knew it was probably a fraud. I then called the company and they informed me someone had hacked his email account.

- We get these all the time. The closest we got to releasing the wire was caught when the second approver reviewed the backup and noticed the initial email requesting the wire was BEC. The email thread was long and was forwarded multiple times before it landed in AP, so it had taken on an air of legitimacy. Once the whole thread was reviewed, however, the BEC email was obvious.

- They emailed a payment request pretending to be a new Administrator

- Spoof email/lots of typos in the message

- CFO verified the request by phone with the CEO.

- We make immediate phone calls to the "requestor" (i.e. president of company) and ask if she has initiated a wire request.

- Funds were Ach'd out and a follow up to the customer was made to make sure received, and they didn't know what we were talking about.

- Just knowledge of the potential for fraud alerted me that it looked suspicious.

- Every invoice needs to be approved by someone other than the person requesting the order

- We have controls in place. The email looked to come from our CFO but didn't follow our process.

- Associate reported to Manager who confirmed authenticity through IT Department.

- Individuals are aware of this fraud so they were skeptical of the requests.

- The signature block in the email was not the correct

- Contacted the CEO directly on his company provided cell phone (he was travelling overseas at the time of the attempt).

- CEO requested wire transfer to the CFO via email. CFO requested additional supporting documentation from CEO whose email account was taken over. CFO noticed the response to her email request indicated the email account was actually being spoofed with an alternate address.

- Spam blocker software

- Control system--got CFO to look over the email and catch the wrong email address

- We were vigilant.

- As a smaller company, it is well known who the CEO or CFO would approach to ask for a wire. As the AP Specialist, all such requests must first go by me, then by two others before it would have transmitted. We have enough processes in place to detect fraud, and enough training on what to look for, that we have been successful in catching any fraudulent requests thus far.

- Suspicious email address or request.

- Not a company email address

- Talking directly with the CEO before proceeding with the wire transfer.

BEC Fraud: Changes Made

We also asked what changes companies made after encountering a BEC attempt. Here are some of the tactics our members are now using.

- Do not wire unless we personally speak to the CEO prior to transferring the funds

- We already have a process in place with our IT department. We send the email to a special IT email address and they block that address and any others like it.

- We investigated this thoroughly and were able to get to the bottom of it before any refund was sent. So, our processes worked

- Just warning from IT to not respond to emails like this

- All such emails are sent directly to our IT dept to verify sender.

- Emphasized to follow procedures in place - if in doubt, call CEO to verify request.

- We report the email address to the IT department and that flag those domains

- No new processes, just a keener eye kept on emails.

- The practices were in place to catch the fraud and they worked.

- No changes, just a reminder to watch the emails for such requests closely to all of AP and a congrats to the processor that made the catch.

- Verify via telephone with the requesting party even if it appears to be legit

- Our IT department put in place a filter that now amends emails that are coming from an external source.

- All wire requests must be approved by the controller who personally verifies with the requester via telephone.

- Wire requests always require verbal confirmation

- Continue to remind employees to question all e-mails.

- Adding "phish alert" to emails so that IT dept can investigate emails in question.

- Additional training required to inform staff. IT testing to gather our % success of identifying fraudulent emails.

- Training was rolled out to all staff and IT now flags all external emails with a message to exercise caution

- We are alerted to flag our IT department whenever we receive a strange/unfamiliar email

- BEC emails are so atypical of how we do wires, that they are obvious to the AP staff. When received, we share them among the AP staff so everyone knows what they look like. Our email system also flags and quarantines emails where the sender name is in the firm but the sending email address is not their firm email address. Lastly, any atypical or large dollar wires are confirmed either by phone or a separate newly initiated email thread. It also takes two authorized individuals to initiate and release wires, so both of those folks are looking at the backup.

- All special payment requests from Admin must come to AP Manager

- We always verify an e-mail request for payment in person or by phone with the CFO and CEO.

- We verify with customer beforehand,

- Communicating the threat and the need to be diligent.

- No changes, just be diligent

- Fraud Bulletins issued Company Wide to ALL email users.

- Report all suspicious emails to our IT department

- No changes, just warning to all about the attempt and continue policy of requesting additional support (verification) for any payment requests.

- Just remind others that this can happen

- CFO met face-to-face with everyone in accounting to alert them and instruct them that no money is to be transferred out of the organization without a face-to-face discussion with the CFO.

Vendor Impersonation Fraud.

The most common type of vendor impersonation fraud is crooks sending emails requesting a change of bank account where electronic payments are sent. Pretending to be a representative of the vendor they supply a new bank account number, which of course, they control. We asked about this issue in our Newer & Less-common Payment Fraud Survey earlier this year.

Uncovering the Fraud. We asked survey respondents how the fraud was uncovered. The most common methods included being notified by the vendor that payment was not received (ugly) and finding out during the verification process before the payment was sent. (much better). But these were not the only paths to discovering these frauds. Other methods included:

- Reconciliation of bank account

- Recognized that the request was unusual and did not follow our standard procedures

- Vendor notified us that impersonation was taking place.

- Bank identified

- Treasury found it in time to stop the vendor payment.

- Our banks security scans found a look alike dummy email address for me. No fraud had been attempted at that time. I forwarded the info to our IT Dept and further investigation found the source of the fake domain email address and a fake web site linked to it.

- Emails were getting suspicious, a phone call to the Supplier confirmed their email account had been hijacked

- The receiving bank contacted us

- Suspicion of the email request

Changes Made. We also asked what changes organizations made after discovering a fraud. Of course, at that point, many were convinced of the advisability of verifying change of bank account requests. Other changes reported by survey participants included:

- Additional controls and review of requests from suppliers wanting to change their banking information for EFT (ACH) payments

- Before we make any changes, we require the vendor to provide the last 3 deposit amounts and dates of the deposits that they received from us to verify they are the vendor.

- Strengthened our policy for updating information

- We implemented an independent confirmation of the request by obtaining the company's phone number from another source, and calling independently to confirm the requested change

- Created teams to help identify weaknesses.

- We use double approvals in our online banking functions and confirm out of the ordinary wire/payment requests by a known phone number or in person.

- Require a voided check and/or letter from bank showing account ownership. Also require that they provide the previous bank info.

- We always verify changes to bank accounts and addresses using a different form of communication. If the vendor sends an email, we call using a phone number on an older invoice to verify the change of information. If they call, we confirm using email information we have on file.

Recommended Best Practice. All supplier bank account changes are confirmed through a known (on-file) contact phone number or email prior to the changes being made. Most of the time it will turn out the request is legitimate. But the few times are not can cost an organization a huge amount.

Some Newer Frauds

The innovativeness of fraudsters continues to astound. One of the issues that has become apparent is that one of the best ways to help combat the threats we face is to ensure that everyone in the organization is educated and updated about the newest schemes. While not every scam will be targeted at every employee, enough of them cut a wide swath, that it is advisable that everyone is updated. Let's take a look at some of the more common ones sweeping businesses across the country. Please feel free to copy and share this with anyone you feel may be impacted.

- **The Date Game**. How do you write the date, on checks and elsewhere? If you are like me, for example, for last Christmas, you might have written 12/25/19. In 2020, writing the date like that could present future problems. Why? Because if you wrote, 12/25/20 and someone wanted to alter the date, they could simply add two digits. So, 12/25/20 could easily become 12/25/2019 or 12/25/2021, depending on what the fraudster needed. So, even though it might look odd, in the year 2020, write out the year using four digits. So, Christmas day will be 12/25/2020.
  Primary Target: Anyone who signs documents or writes checks

- **The Gift Card Game**. This fraud is also referred to as Boss Impersonation Fraud. In this fraud, an employee receives an email (or text) that looks like it came from their immediate supervisor requesting they purchase some gift cards. The amounts typically range from $500 to $2,000. This fraud usually involves several

emails. Once the gift cards are purchased, the crook (still impersonating the boss) asks the employee to scratch off the silver coating on the back and either send the numbers or take a picture of the back and send it to them. They use this information to cash in the gift cards.
Primary Target: Anyone, especially lower level employees.

- **The W-2 Game.** This is a slightly different fraud, which is probably why so many fell for it, initially. It involves a request for personnel data (usually, but not always, the W-2 file) purportedly from high-level executive. This fraud has gotten so bad the IRS now recommends that all requests from high-level executives for personnel information be confirmed before the data is sent. They also recommend that two people review the request before it is sent.
Primary Target: Payroll and HR, as well as anyone with access to personnel or tax records.

- **The Voice Game**. The latest variant on the Rush wire transfer requests involves using AI-enhanced voice technology to request a wire transfer over the phone. Since the person "thinks" they recognize the voice on the other end of the phone, they go ahead and execute the transfer. Verify all wire requests, and other phone requests for money, even if you recognize the voice on the other end of the phone.
Primary Target: Whoever normally handles wire transfers or change of bank account requests

- **The Change Game**. New frauds abound, in ways most of us never imagined. Therefore, any time a request for anything is received that requests anything outside the normal process, verify it. This might include a drop shipment to a customer that has never received one, a request for ACH payment from someone who only would accept checks, a request for sensitive information by a senior level executive who has never had a need for that type of data etc.

Primary Target: Anyone

Fraud is a frequent topic on the AP Now podcast. It is one of the places where we disseminate information about new frauds. You can listen to these podcasts at https://www.ap-now.com/public/AP-Now-Podcast.cfm or wherever you normally listen to podcasts (including the purple podcast button on your iPhone). AP Now has put a number of its fraud protection podcasts on one page. You can access them at https://www.ap-now.com/public/Short-Explanations-of-Newer-Frauds-audio.cfm

Other Payment Frauds and How They Can Be Prevented

In going through the data from a recent AP Now payment fraud survey, one of the things that we noticed – aside from the horrendous number of companies being targeted with BEC fraud – was the number of innovative ways crooks are still trying to defraud companies. Some were new while others are simply variants of old frauds. What follows is a look at some of the more common, along with ways the fraud can be stopped.

- **The Fraud**: A former employee found that his card wasn't terminated and chose to use it. It isn't clear how he discovered this – whether by accident or not. But it demonstrates why companies have to be thorough in their fraud prevention and detection protocols.
  How to Prevent: Cards should be collected from the employee upon his or her termination. Additionally, and more importantly, the bank should be notified immediately that the card is cancelled. Otherwise a crafty employee will simply write down the card number, expiration date and the code.

- **The Fraud**: Hackers changed direct deposit information on employees. Over 50 employees had their paychecks go to an account other than their own.
  How to Prevent: This is a version of a corporate account takeover or compromise. Care needs to be taken when clicking on links in emails and downloading attachments. Also, employees should not be visiting questionable websites using company computers.

- **The Fraud**: Ransom ware. This occurs when one of your employees is duped into clicking on an infected popup advertisement on their visits an infected website. However, instead of just trying to trick you into buying fake antivirus software. The crooks hold your computer hostage and attempt to extort payment.
  How to Prevent: Make sure your employees understand employees understand what is involved. Prevention is the same as above. Also

enable popup blockers. They are a favorite of fraudsters trying to perpetrate this fraud.

- **The Fraud**: Employees receive an email which is phishing asking for their password. Unfortunately, it was reported that the employee in question was fooled into thinking the email was legitimate and provided their passwords. There were several reported instances of this.
  How to Prevent: Employee education is critical. They should know that no reputable firm would ask for a password.

- **The Fraud**: An individual got hold of someone else's check. This gave them bank account information and they set up an online payment to payments for their cable and phone bills. The amounts ranged from $150 to $350. This went on for some time.
  How to Prevent: The fraud was caught while doing the daily bank reconciliation and the matter turned over to law enforcement. However, if positive pay had been used on this account, the fraud would have been uncovered immediately.

- **The Fraud**: More than one respondent reported they are starting to see several checks being deposited via mobile deposit system and then taken to a check cashing place effectively getting paid a second time.
  How to Prevent: The best way to prevent this type of fraud is to not pay with paper checks. Using positive pay will protect your company as well, although it doesn't help the check cashing facility that cashed the check. Positive pay, or payee name positive pay will protect your organization.

- **The Fraud**: A vendor check was sent to the old address and new tenant attempted to cash/deposit the check at the bank the check was drawn on. There were a number of variations of this reported where someone other than the intended party managed to get hold of a check and cashed it.
  How to Prevent: Payee name positive pay will protect your organization as will reducing the number of paper checks issued. This is one reason why it is recommended that checks be kept carefully and not taken to the mailroom until it is time for the mail to be taken to the post office.

- **The Fraud**: We have received multiple invoices that are fraudulent requests for money. Many are related to office supply products such as toner cartridges. This is an old fraud that is still being perpetrated, probably because it works enough of the time to make it profitable – for the crooks!
  How to Prevent: Require a PO number or name of a requisitioner on every invoice. If you receive one without that information, return it to the vendor explaining your requirement. Some of the phony vendors will go away at that point. Others won't. If they continue threatening and demanding turn the tables on them. Tell them you are going to contact the attorney general in the state they are located. The odds are high they will not be located in the same state as your company, but don't let that stop you.

- **The Fraud**: A stopped payment check was voided and reissued, but both checks cashed at a check cashing establishment.
  How to Prevent: Use positive pay, or even better if it is available, payee name positive pay. When you issue the stop payment, check the positive pay file. If it is outstanding make sure you remove the check from the positive pay file. That protects your organization. If you know the party who mislead you, inform them you will be turning the matter over to the police – and do it.

- **The Fraud**: Phone call requesting bank account information and DOB, name, address, social security number and telephone number
  How to Prevent: Hopefully, your employees are smart enough not to fall for this. Employee education is critical.

As you can see, the crooks are alive and well finding new ways to defraud your organization. That doesn't mean they've given up the old ways; they still work. It just means there are more avenues available to them and the business community has to continue to be vigilant in order to protect itself.

Hiding Places: Looking for Fraud in All the Right Places

Usually when we talk about fraud in this publication, we focus on payment fraud. We also focus on tight internal controls and appropriate segregation of duties. By no means do we mean to underestimate the importance of those issues. But, unfortunately for the business world, there are other places where fraud can be uncovered in the payment arena. In this section we will look at ten of those that touch the accounts payable function and show you how to uncover the fraud hiding in the details of the transaction.

Hiding Place #1: Your vendor complaints. Do you investigate vendor complaints thoroughly, especially the ones that sound outlandish? Sometimes the complaints not only are legitimate they are a result of an employee playing games for their own enrichment. Of course, the perpetration of the fraud could be by the vendor so don't jump to conclusions right away.

Hiding Place #2: Your customer complaints. Just like the grievances of your vendors, your customers may have legitimate gripes caused by an ongoing fraud being committed by one of your employees. So, follow up and investigate closely. And, as with the vendor issues, it could be the customer trying to pull the wool over your eyes.

Hiding Place #3: Increased purchases from a particular vendor. An increase might reflect a kickback to one of your purchasing executives. To determine if the increase is substantial, compare average monthly purchases with the current month's purchases. Also, look at the prices being charged. Are they in line with what other vendors are charging? You might also want to consider whether another supplier of this produce has gone out of business or if a contract has been signed to purchase at a superior price. There's a lot of investigation that needs to go into this issue before you can determine if a fraud is in play.

Hiding Place #4: Questionable documentation. Unless there is an obvious reason, documentation for invoices should be original copies. If the documentation is obvious copies, you can question why. There may be a good reason, it could be a duplicate payment or worse, if could be fraud. The starting point is questioning the problematical documentation.

Hiding Place #5: Unusual endorsements on checks. If you get your checks returned from your bank, you can quickly thumb through the checks to see if any stand out as questionable. This might be an individual's signature on a corporate check. Most use a deposit stamp. If you don't get the checks, just the images, take a quick scan to see if anything jumps out and hits you as odd.

Hiding Place #6: Odd cancellation of vendor invoices. Some organizations cancel paper invoices after processing them. This might be with a hand stamp that says paid or with one of those machines that actually puts little holes through the invoices. If you use these approaches and find one with odd cancelations on it, look for a duplicate payment or worse, fraud.

Hiding Place #7: Altered or modified invoices. It's one thing to mark an invoice and pay a smaller amount than is due. It is a whole other issue if the invoice is marked up and a higher amount is put on the invoice for payment. Most organizations would not pay such an invoice requiring the vendor to send a revised invoice. Any invoice with handwritten or changes should be investigated closely. What's more, it is not a good idea to allow handwritten changes. For even if the change is legitimate, it sets a bad precedent and potentially opens the door for future fraud.

Hiding Place #8: Unusual payees. Hopefully a check written out to cash would set bells off for everyone reading this. But, more than that, checks other than payroll or expense reimbursement should also raise a red flag and be immediately investigated. The documentation for such checks, if they are legitimate, should be quite thorough and signed off by a senior manager.

Hiding Place #9: A different payee on the check register than the actual check. Clearly, this would be difficult to identify since most bank reconciliations are done by check number and dollar amount. Also, this problem is unlikely to occur with computer generated checks. If Rush checks are manually generated this might be possible. It is also the way most check fraud is committed today. The crook gets the check and knowing the organization uses positive pay, alters the payee name only. All differences should be investigated immediately.

Hiding Place #10: Unexpected changes in payables disbursements. This should be investigated immediately. It could be an error or it could be fraud. It needs to be identified and determined if the disbursement is correct. If not, action should be taken to retrieve the funds.

All of the issues discussed above require a thorough investigation before you decide there is fraud and an even more diligent investigation before you resolve who the guilty party is. But identifying the problem is the first step. We've given you some clues on where to look. The ball is now in your court as you decide how to proceed.

Chapter 19: Some Password Best Practices

Given the criminal attempts that are likely to have gone on during the COVID-19 crisis, we thought it appropriate to include a short chapter on passwords. In this section, we'll cover the following:

- Creating a Password Using IRS Guidelines
- Weak Practice: Sharing Passwords
- Updating Passwords Post COVID-19

Strong passwords protect online accounts and digital devices from data theft. But there have been some important changes many people can overlook.

In recent years, cybersecurity experts' recommendations on what constitutes a strong password has changed. They now suggest that people use word phrases that are easy to remember rather than random letters, characters and numbers that cannot be easily recalled.

For example, experts previously suggested something like "PXro#)30," but now suggest a longer phrase like "SomethingYouCanRemember@30." By using a phrase, users don't have to write down their password and expose it to additional risk. Also, people may be more willing to use strong, longer passwords if it's a phrase rather than random characters that are harder to remember.

Protecting access to digital devices is so critical that some now feature fingerprint or facial recognition technology, but passwords remain common for many people.

Creating a Password Using IRS Guidelines

Given the sensitivity of many of these online accounts, people should consider these passwords tips to protect devices or online accounts:

- Use a minimum of eight characters; longer is better.
- Use a combination of letters, numbers and symbols in password phrases, i.e., UsePasswordPhrase@30.
- Avoid personal information or common passwords; use phrases instead.
- Change default or temporary passwords that come with accounts or devices.
- Do not reuse or update passwords. For example, changing Bgood!17 to Bgood!18 is not good enough; use unique usernames and passwords for accounts and devices.
- Do not use email addresses as usernames if that is an option.
- Store any password list in a secure location, such as a safe or locked file cabinet.
- Do not disclose passwords to anyone for any reason.
- When available, a password manager program can help track passwords for numerous accounts.

Whenever it is an option for a password-protected account, users also should opt for a multi-factor authentication process. Many email providers, financial institutions and social media sites now offer customers two-factor authentication protections.

Two-factor authentication helps by adding an extra layer of protection. Often two-factor authentication means the returning user must enter their credentials (username and password) plus another step, such as entering a security code sent via text to a mobile phone. Another example is confirming "yes" to a text to the phone that users are accessing the account on.

The idea behind multi-factor authentication is that a thief may be able to steal usernames and passwords, but it's highly unlikely they also would have access to the mobile phone to receive a security code or confirmation to actually complete the log-in process.

Remember: the IRS will never ask for passwords. And watch out for phishing emails posing as trusted companies seeking passwords.

Source: IRS

Weak Practice: Sharing Passwords

It is quite tempting when an employee is heading out for vacation to ask that employee to share his/her password with another employee who will take over the vacationing employee's responsibility. Resist the temptation. This is a slippery slope and whether sharing a password for a vacation or on a regular basis, it is a bad idea. It completely obliterates the audit trail making it impossible to tell who did what.

Solution: The answer is obvious. When someone needs to take over the responsibilities of another employee, set them up with their own password. When the vacation is over and if you don't need/want that employee to have access, cancel the access. This may be an extra step but it protects your internal controls.

Updating Passwords Post COVID-19

As I write this in the middle of the pandemic, most accounts payable teams are working remotely. After a rough start, most have gotten the payment function up and running and have done so in an admirable fashion. Without a doubt, in a few cases, corners were cut and perhaps passwords shared. Even if they weren't, they may have been given to the IT person who was trying to troubleshoot a computer from a remote location or otherwise compromised.

Therefore, it is recommended upon your return to "normal" working processes that all passwords be updated. And if you incorporated any weak practices, this would be the time to eliminate them. Some examples of commonly used weak practices for creating a password include:

- Using your pet's name
- Using your children or spouse's name
- Using your birthday or wedding anniversary
- Using your address
- A string of consecutive numbers
- A string of consecutive letters (ghijkl12345)
- I love you

- !@#$%^&*() – if you can't figure this one out, look at the symbols above the numbers on your keyboard
- And of course, password

And one other password issue, have you shared your passwords with a significant other and that relationship ended. Even if it ended amicably, change your passwords. You'd be surprised how many people forget to take this step.

Last Recommended Best Password Practice

You know this; but we're going to say it anyway because few take it to heart. Passwords should be changed—don't groan—every few months. All of them. Some folks never change their passwords. Given the number of recent data breaches in recent years, regular changing of passwords should be part of your arsenal of protection.

So, when you return to whatever the new normal will be, change all your passwords.

Chapter 20: A 1099 Action Plan:
Given Changes Coming to 1099 Reporting

Normally, I would not include a chapter on tax reporting in a book of this sort. However, the IRS has made a massive change to the way the 1099 reporting will be done next year. Given that many are in quarantine during the spring of 2020, the changes that need to be made to accommodate this IRS change are not being addressed in some organizations. This is a mistake. So, I've included some information on the issue.

In this section, we investigate the following:

- The Big 1099 Change

- Getting Ready for 1099 Reporting

- Using IRS TIN Matching Properly

The Big 1099 Change

They have introduced two new forms (1099NEC and a new 1099-MISC) which will need to be used for reporting in January 2021. We know from conversations with many of our readers that many organizations have not started making the necessary IT changes to enable reporting.

This will create a ton of extra work in January 2021, for those who wait until that time to make the needed changes. They will also have one year's worth of data to resort. Complicating the matter is the prediction by some experts that the coronavirus could flare up next winter and we could be back sitting at home running our accounts payable function remotely.

Issuing 1099s are stress-inducing enough for most without adding the complication of having to update our systems to accommodate new IRS forms and doing it remotely. This is a recipe for disaster. So, the bottom line is this: If you haven't started your updates, move it to the top of the list when you return to the office.

Getting Ready for 1099 Reporting

Whether you are getting ready to comply with the possible new 1099 rules or just implementing best practices in your current 1099 procedures the process is the same. Those already using best practices in this area are prepared. After all, what's the big deal? All you have to do is collect, track and verify. Of course, those responsible for this task know all too well, collecting W-9s, tracking the process and verifying that the information provided using the IRS TIN Matching program is not as easy as it sounds.

Before You Can Start Your Process

Step 1: Cleanse the master vendor file focusing on:

- Eliminating duplicate vendors

- Deactivating inactive vendors

- Getting a good mailing address, in addition to the bank lock box address many have in their Remit to field.

Step 2: Set up a methodology for tracking the receipt of W-9s. This can be done in your master vendor file, your ERP system or elsewhere. The important issue is that as part of your invoice processing a check be done to ensure a good W-9 has been received. Ideally, this will be automated with your system refusing to schedule the invoice for payment without the requisite TIN information.

Step 3: Sign up to use the IRS TIN Matching program.

Collecting the TIN Information

Step 4: To update your records if you have not collected W-9s in the past, send out letters and/or emails requesting W-9s. Make is easy for your vendors. Let them respond by mail, fax or email.

Step 5: Request a W-9 from new vendors, ideally before the PO is issued but definitely before a payment is made.

Step 6: When new orders are to be placed with existing vendors who have not supplied W-9s, request one. Ideally the vendor should be notified at the time the order is contemplated that the W-9 is required and the PO will not be issued until the W-9 has been received.

Tracking Your TIN Collection Efforts

Step 7: Track the receipt of the W-9s.

Step 8: Follow up with those who do not respond.

Verifying Your TIN Data

Step 9: Run information provided on the W-9through the IRS TIN Matching Program before making the payment.

Step 10: Follow up with any vendor whose data was rejected

Concluding Thoughts

This is a process that best practice organizations have been using. For them it is nothing new. Make it a standard part of your invoice processing procedures regardless of what action Congress takes.

Using IRS TIN Matching Properly

The IRS TIN Matching is a free service offered by the IRS. It is an online interactive service offered to payers or their authorized agents. IRS TIN Matching Program does as its name suggests. It compares the TIN/Name combinations provided with information held by the IRS on its tax filing records. Organizations may use it to verify information for income subject to backup withholding and reported on Forms 1099-B, DIV, INT, MISC, OID and/or PATR.

This matching can be done online interactively for up to 25 entries at a time or in a bulk basis for up to 100,000 entries. If the latter is used the information is returned 24 hours later.

TIN Matching, under no circumstances, should be used as a phishing expedition to try and determine the correct information. If the IRS determines you are phishing, you will be kicked off the system.

The primary benefit of use of TIN Matching is a significant reduction in the number of B-Notices. Organizations that start using TIN Matching report the elimination of between 97% and 100% of all their B-Notices.

Best Practice: All information provided by vendors on a W-9 should be verified using IRS TIN Matching before the first purchase order is given. If there is a mismatch corrected information should be requested and run through TIN Matching again.

Almost Best Practice: All information provided by vendors on a W-9 should be verified using IRS TIN Matching before the first payment is made. If there is a mismatch corrected information should be requested and run through TIN Matching again.

Special Pointers for Accounts Payable: There is really no excuse for not using the IRS TIN Matching program. Anecdotal evidence suggests that the most common reason for not using TIN Matching is executive reluctance. This unwillingness stems from the fact that when registering the organization to use TIN Matching the executive is required to supply his or her social security number as well as their AGI (adjusted gross income) from their last tax return filed with the IRS.

It is not uncommon to hear executives complain, "I'm not giving them that information." In reality, they are not giving the IRS any information it does not already have. The IRS only requests this information so it can identify that the individual signing the company up for TIN Matching is who they say they are. It is for identification purposes only.

Chapter 21: Payment Audits

Even in the best of times, at best practice organizations, an occasional duplicate or erroneous payment slips through. Whether this is because the vendor in question went out of their way to trick the customer into paying twice is beside the point. It happens. And during the COVID-19 pandemic it was definitely not the best of times and more than occasionally, best practices went by the wayside.

Thus, it is important that every organization conduct a payment audit when work returns to whatever will be considered normal. Without a doubt, there will have been more duplicate payments made than in the prior year. If you have the resources, before calling in the experts (who you have to pay), consider doing a statement audit yourself and recover what you can.

In this section, we take a look at the following issues:

- Statement Audits

- Best Practices for Payment Audits

- Caveats

- Debunking Three Common Recovery Myths

- Hiring a Duplicate Payment Audit Firm

Statement Audits; Recovering Your Open Credits Yourself

The first move in the recovery process is to recognize this issue. The following steps should help you recover most, if not all, of your outstanding open credits.

Step 1: Review all accounts at least once a year. Begin by requesting the vendor send a statement showing all open activity. Make sure the vendor understands you want credits included. Otherwise, some may take advantage of the nasty feature in their software that allows them to suppress vendor credits when printing statements. Every account should be reviewed at least once a year, as credits are not always where you think they'd be.

Step 2: Identify those accounts with significant recoveries and schedule them for quarterly reviews. There's no sense leaving your funds sitting any longer than necessary. Quarterly reviews will help. Some even get monthly statements, if credit experience warrants it.

Step 3: Once the credits have been identified either request funds be returned or ask for a credit memo. Make sure you staff on top of this issue, tracking credits requested and credits used. Some simply take the credit.

Step 4: Re-solicit those vendors who have not supplied recent statements. Just because you ask for the statements, doesn't mean all vendors will comply. Politely, but firmly, remind vendors who haven't sent copies of requested statements that you are waiting for them. Realistically though, be aware that it is unlikely you'll get 100% of the statements you request, no matter how persistent you are.

Step 5: Set up a regular schedule for requesting statements (and reviewing them) as part of your accounts payable procedures. It's not enough to request and receive the statements; the value comes in reviewing them and recovering the funds owed your organization.

Step 6: Keep track of all your recoveries, along with the reasons the credits were created in the first place. This information is critical to plugging the gaps in your processes.

Step 7: Analyze the data related to your recoveries to determine where you can tighten your processes to ensure future credits are not created. It's not enough to simply recover your open credits; you want to stop them from being created, where possible. It's probably not possible to completely eliminate them, but you can make a serious dent in them by studying the issues that lead to their creation.

Step 8: Periodically review new data to identify new places where you may have weaknesses in your processes that result in the creation of vendor credits. The analytical process is not a one-shot project but one that should be repeated every year or two to identify new problem spots.

The Issue

The issue of payment audits can cause heated debate among professionals in accounts payable. Only about one in three organizations have one of these audits done on a regular basis. A payment audit involves a third-party firm reviewing the payment activity with an eye towards identifying and recovering duplicate and erroneous payments. These audits typically also involve the third party recovering unidentified open credits.

There are many benefits associated with having a payment audit done. Clearly there is the financial gain of the funds recovered during the audit. These are reduced by the contingency percentage typically taken by the audit firm. Additionally, the firm should prepare a management report highlighting any weaknesses in your existing process. This report should be scoured thoroughly and the weak spots identified should be fixed.

Too often people boast that the reason they don't have an audit done is they never make a duplicate payment. Unfortunately, even the best run organization makes a mistake from time to time. What's more, if the person is correct and no duplicate payments are ever made, then the cost for the audit will be minimal, assuming an agency working on a contingency basis is selected.

Another reason people sometimes give for not having an audit done is the expense. They claim the firms charge too much. Let's look at a simple example and see if that theory holds water. Let's assume the audit firm finds and recovers $1 million for the client. In this hypothetical case, the audit firm gets a 25% contingency fee, leaving the client with $750,000 of the $1 million. But, if the firm is not hired, how much will the client recover? How much does it cost not to hire the audit firm? If you are saying nothing, I do not agree. I believe it cost the client $750,000 that will never be recovered unless an audit firm is hired.

This brings up one last issue, or dirty little secret, related to recovery audits. Many people have asked, "well doesn't the vendor return duplicate payments?" And the answer to that question is "most don't." About 1 in 100 vendors will return a duplicate payment without any prompting. The next issue raised is about unclaimed property. And, the answer is yes, the vendor should be turning this money over to the states as part of its unclaimed property reporting – three, four or five years later. However, most don't. They either write it off to miscellaneous income or use it to cover unearned early payment discounts, unauthorized deductions or discrepant invoices. At the end of the day, unless you hire a third party firm or set up a separate unit to recover duplicate and erroneous payments, most of your money held with vendors will be lost.

Best Practice

As suggested above, you can do some easy processes to strip off the low-hanging fruit in terms of duplicate and erroneous payments and open vendor credits. If you have adequate staff, you can request quarterly statements from vendors and recover open credits yourself. Once you've done everything you possibly can, call in the pros and see what they can find. Ideally this should be an ongoing process so the vendors don't have a chance to "use" your open credits to clean up their books.

Caveats

Many accounts payable departments are reluctant to have a payment audit done for fear they will be blamed for any funds recovered by the audit firm. This is not fair for often the errors are a result of poor practices elsewhere in the procure-to-pay chain. By getting the management report you will be able to identify these problems. Accounts payable can also make sure that vendors send credit memos directly to accounts payable. Too often they go to purchasing who then throws them away or files them not realizing what they are.

Finally, there is the unclaimed property issue. As mentioned above, these items should be turned over to the state and sometimes they are. In fact, audit firms know that they can start their recovery by reclaiming funds turned over to the state. This is something you can do yourself, assuming you are currently reporting and remitting your organization's unclaimed property. If you are not, filing a claim is like waving a red flag in front of a bull. It will trigger an audit. The amount you recover will be small in comparison to the pain and cost of an audit, when you are not in compliance. Of course, the best practice advice in this arena is to get in compliance. This issue should be kept in mind when hiring the audit firm. If you don't want them recovering funds from the state, tell them this is NOT to be part of the audit.

Debunking Three Common Recovery Myths

Most experts believe that only one in three organizations have third-party duplicate payment audits performed so the odds that your organization is among them are not good. This is unfortunate because this not only leaves money on the table but also results in continual cash leakage in your procure-to-pay cycle. The truth is a good audit firm will tell you where the weaknesses are so you can plug them and stop the losses.

We wondered why so few companies have audits done so we asked a number of them about their reluctance. What we discovered are several serious misconceptions about audits. Whether our respondents actually believe these explanations or simply don't want to face the bigger issues is not clear. Here's a look at three of the common reasons we heard for not having audits done along with a look at what's wrong with that reasoning.

#1 Duplicate Payments Are Returned

"If I make a duplicate payment, the vendor will return it," said more than one professional we spoke with. While this is occasionally true, it only happens in very rare circumstances. What's more, some of the duplicate payments that *are* returned aren't returned to the accounts payable department but to the CFO or some other high-level executive with a snide note from the vendor. This is embarrassing for the executive and not a good thing for those responsible for ensuring financial integrity of the disbursement process.

While it is true that certain duplicates do get credited appropriately to the account and future payments reduced correspondingly, these instances are few. This applies mainly to utilities, credit card payments, and the like. What it does not apply to is payments made by check after an original credit card payment. For the most part duplicate payments, when finally identified, sit as credits on the vendor's books rarely reported back to the paying organization.

Most experts estimate that over half of all duplicate payments are never recovered by the paying organization unless an audit is undertaken.

#2 Reliance on Accounting System

"We can't make a duplicate payment because our system won't accept a duplicate invoice number," claim a number of other managers we spoke with. They say this with great confidence and they are correct. What they have not factored into this equation is the creativity of their processors.

Without exception, whenever I speak with processors at organizations relying on this control, they share a little secret. They get around the invoice number restriction by simply adding a space, period, asterisk, or some other character to the invoice number forcing the system to recognize it as a new invoice number. Thus the invoice number control is of little use.

#3 The Expense

A number of professionals report they don't have duplicate payment audits because they are just too expensive. And there's some truth in that. Let's assume for purposes of this article that an organization has $1 million of duplicate payments and it has to pay the audit firm a 25% contingency fee to recover the money. That *is* expensive; $250,000 is a lot of money.

But that's only half the picture. If the firm doesn't hire the firm to recover its duplicates, what is the cost? Some might claim the answer is nothing. We believe in our hypothetical example, the cost of not hiring an audit firm is $750,000—and that is far more expensive than paying the $250,000!

AP Now is a huge advocate of audit recoveries done on a contingency basis. The best firms provide insights into how you can tighten your processes to prevent duplicate payments in the future—and since they work on a contingency basis, if they find nothing, they get nothing.

Hiring a Duplicate Payment Audit Firm

Even firms employing every best practice in the world do see the occasional duplicate payment slip through the net. To find the annoying critters that slithered through your highly-guarded payment fortress, the last line of defense in the war against them is to hire a duplicate payment audit firm, also referred to as a recovery audit firm. When you get ready to hire such a firm, the 20 questions shown in the accompanying table will help you narrow the field and select the recovery group best suited to your company.

References

While there is no right or wrong answer to any of the questions asked, the responses will help you form a picture of the audit firm and how it will mesh with your organization. Be sure to ask for references from all firms you are considering hiring but take them with a huge grain of salt. Few will offer references, after all, from jobs that did not go well or where the client wasn't satisfied.

If you belong to an industry group, ask at your regional meetings for both recommendations and names of firms where the audits have not gone well. But remember, occasionally a job doesn't go well because the company in question can't or doesn't provide the information the auditors need to conduct a satisfactory audit.

The Hourly Rate vs. Contingency Fee Debate

Expect an interesting discussion when you ask if the employees of the firm work on an hourly rate or a contingency fee. This is a hotly contested issue in the industry with strong feelings on both sides.

The main issue, as you might imagine, is that when folks are paid on a contingency basis, they are less likely to aggressively pursue small-dollar transactions. This is where the bulk of the duplicate payments are likely to occur but not where the lion's share of the recovered dollars come from.

The Consultant's Report

Most good audit firms will provide a report at the end of the engagement identifying the weaknesses in your processes that allowed the duplicates to slip through. This is extremely valuable and should be used to fix your processes. Remember it comes from an unbiased third party.

Unfortunately, many of the auditors I speak to reveal—off the record, of course—that their clients rarely take the actions they recommend. This provides another earning opportunity for the auditor a year or two down the road.

Insist on getting the report and then use it to reduce duplicate payments in the future. Often it contains advice you have already been cautioned about, either from your staff or accountants, but have never implemented. It will also improve your Sarbanes-Oxley compliance.

Once the decision to hire a firm has been made, use the questions in the accompanying table to help you select the firm that best meets your needs—and then follow the advice they give in their consultant's report.

20 Questions to Help You Select the Perfect Recovery Firm

1) Do they have experience in your industry? Industry experience, while not crucial, is desirable as the auditors arrive knowing which vendors are likely to cause duplicate payments.

2) Will the firm provide a report at the end showing the weaknesses in your process? As discussed in the related article, this should be a requirement for any firm you consider hiring.

3) Does the agency work on a contingency fee or hourly rate? There is no right or wrong answer to this question. It is mostly a matter of what you are comfortable with.

4) What is the smallest recovery they pursue? While it is not realistic to expect the auditors to pursue every last dollar, those with high thresholds should be viewed with some caution unless you make very few small-dollar payments. For most organizations, a threshold of $250 — $500 is reasonable.

5) Will they reduce their rates for large recoveries? While most organizations are willing to pay a 25% recovery fee for a $500 duplicate payment, they are not willing to pay that on a $500,000 duplicate. In fact, this is the issue that prevents many people from hiring a recovery firm in the first place. Ask for a reduction in fees. While most won't offer one, if asked they will comply.

6) How much can you expect to receive based on their experience with organizations similar to yours? Of course the answer to this should be taken with a large measure of skepticism too. There is no real way to know. Unless you have very poor controls in place, the answer should be around

.5%, i.e. $5,000 per $1,000,000 of payables. Obviously, those with good controls will have a lower number.

7) How long has the audit firm been in business? If the length of time is minimal, ask how long the principals have been in the industry. They will probably offer this information if they haven't been in business for that long. This isn't necessarily a bad thing, for they may be willing to take a lower recovery fee than those organizations with a big roster of clients.

8) How many full-time employees does it have? This is an indicator of the quality of people who are likely to work your account. If the audit firm routinely hires temps, your recoveries may not be as high as they would under different circumstances.

9) Are the employees paid on a contingency or hourly rate? There is no right or wrong answer to this question. While those paid on a contingency basis are more likely to focus on your higher-dollar items, they are also likely to be more aggressive.

10) What is the background of the principals of the organization? This will give you an idea of their understanding of the industry. It is important that they have worked in the industry or related industries for a good deal of time. If not, they should have some very senior employees who have.

11) What is the background of the employees who will work your case? You want at least one or two experienced professionals on your account. You do not want to be the organization given a bunch of temps because the audit firm took on more clients than it could handle. This doesn't happen often but it does on occasion so check.

12) If you have a lot of freight, advertising, utility billings, postage, and telecom billings ask if the firm has specialized experience in those arenas. These areas involve extreme minutiae and as such, specialized knowledge. Expect to pay more for these audits than you would a straight accounts payable duplicate payment audit. Get references and inquire about the background of the people who will work your case.

13) How much of your staff time will be taken up with the audit? Most recovery audit firms take very little of your staff time, but some is generally required. Find out ahead of time so you don't end up with poor recoveries because you did not allocate adequate staff to help where needed.

14) Will the audit firm need office space in your location or is the bulk of the work done offsite?

15) What are the technical capabilities of the firm? Much of the analytical work is done today using technology. This helps the firm identify potential duplicates quickly and focus on the recovery work. Have some discussion around this topic to determine the level of technical expertise you are hiring.

16) Will the audit firm do second audits? Each audit firm uses its own proprietary routines to identify duplicates. Few can find them all. It would just take too long. Thus, for large firms, a second audit is recommended.

17) What are their rates for secondary audits? Expect the rates for the secondary audit to be higher, perhaps as much as 50%. This is because the cream, or easy finds, has been taken by the primary audit. Make sure to tell the secondary auditor who did your primary audit. There is a very good reason for this. Auditors know who uses routines similar to their own and so know where they will be able to do a good audit and where they won't. Respect their decision not to pursue an audit when you tell them who did your primary audit.

18) How/when does the firm expect to be paid? Does it expect payment when it identifies the duplicate or when you are actually credited for the amount owed? Obviously, you do not want to pay the audit firm until you have either been paid or issued a credit by your vendors.

19) If you decide not to pursue a duplicate (which you might do for a variety of reasons) does the auditor still expect to be compensated? Technically, they have a right to be paid but many will defer if pursuing the duplicate might put you in an embarrassing position such as, say, pursuing a duplicate from a company owned by someone on your board of directors.

20) How long does the auditor expect the audit to take and when can they start? This information will help you plan for any staffing and space requirements. Also, if you need the recoveries within a certain fiscal period, it is crucial you select a firm that can meet your time constraints.

Chapter 22: Dynamic Discounting

The COVID-19 crisis exacerbated cash flow issues for more than a few organizations. Those that were in impacted industries as well as those that were already struggling found themselves in an untenable position. The same was true for many other organizations who found that some of their suppliers were having trouble getting payments issued, either because they were heavily reliant on paper checks or because they were having their own cash flow difficulties.

A few generous companies, with deep pockets, have taken this opportunity to launch dynamic discounting programs or offer seller financing to their customers. These new programs are filling a void in the market.

In this section, we take a look at the following:

- What dynamic discounting means

- How it works

- Why you might consider it

Dynamic discounting is the answer to the age-old dilemma facing many companies and their suppliers. The vendor wants to be paid quickly while the customer does everything in its power to hold onto the payment until the last possible moment. In recent years the problem has been exacerbated as companies extend payment terms, partially in response to a lousy economy, partially because they can get away with it. Often this is done without the concurrence of the vendor. This practice damages vendor relations.

Definition

Dynamic discounting is an agreement between a buyer and supplier whereby payment for invoices is made early in return for a reduced price or discount. The pact includes the right to vary the discount according to the date of early payment. As you might imagine, earlier payment dates translate into greater discounts. The discounting agreement spells out the relationship between the number of days early and the discount.

Often, but not always, a third party stands between the two providing the financing that makes the early payment possible.

The most common form of dynamic discounting is the early payment discount offered by some suppliers; with 2/10 net 30 being frequently offered. But there are many variations depending on industry and other factors. Dynamic discounting, when used effectively, allows all parties meet their unique needs; there's no one-size fits all approach as there is with traditional early payment discounting.

Payment Problems

There are numerous issues that sometimes make paying on time difficult. Historically, it hasn't always been easy for buyers to actually pay early, even if they wished to take advantage of early payment discounts. For starters, they may not have the cash flow to do so. But even, if they do there are logistical issues that sometime prevent that from happening. Just getting the invoices delivered to the right place and getting them processed quickly can be problematic. And, if there are discrepancies, that throws a real monkey wrench in the timetable.

On the other side of the coin, many suppliers have difficulty obtaining credit and their financial situation is exacerbated by late payments on the part of their customers. Dynamic discounting helps with this issue as it is typically based on the credit of the buyer. This particular type of financing is particularly popular when you have a large entity with a good credit rating purchasing from many smaller companies. For this to work, the provider of the financing, when a third party is used, for the discounting has to be assured the payment will actually be made.

Background: Early Payment Discounts

Early payment discounts have been around for a long time. They are coveted by most accounts payable groups as they represent a very attractive rate of return in exchange for an early payment on an invoice. However, they are offered at the discretion of the seller and there is usually little the customer can do to get a vendor who doesn't offer early pay discounts to offer them.

That's because as good a rate of return as the early pay discount is for the purchaser, it is an equally poor rate for the seller. As most readers are aware, 2/10 net 30 is equivalent to a 36% rate of return in exchange for paying 20 days early. This is definitely a zero-sum game and across the board sellers seem reluctant to start programs, if they do not already have one in place.

This is not to say they don't want to be paid early. They most definitely do. They just don't want to pay 36% to get it.

The Flip Approach

Dynamic discounting takes the age-old practice of offering early pay discounts and turns it upside down. In this scenario, it is the buyer who offers the seller the option to get paid early – at a discount. At least in the current interest rate environment, the discounts are nowhere near as large as those traditionally offered with early payment discounts.

Dynamic discounting is an agreement between a buyer and seller. In exchange for a price reduction, the purchaser agrees to pay earlier than the normal payment terms. The size of the discount depends upon how early the payment is made.

The Basic Requirement

For dynamic discounting to work effectively for your vendors, invoices must be processed and approved promptly. For without quick turnaround on invoices, a dynamic invoicing program loses much of its value.

Thus you will often see dynamic discounting offered in conjunction with an e-invoicing program. In fact, some of the third party e-invoicing service providers are integrating a dynamic invoicing feature in their product. This is not to say the e-invoicing service provider is offering to fund the discounting program. That needs to be worked out.

How It Works

The vendor decides whether or not to take advantage of the dynamic discounts offered. The vendor makes the call, invoice by invoice. So, they can use it when they want and decline at other times. Some will use it seasonally to smooth out their cash flow and others will use it depending on the rate offered. Still others may choose to never use it.

Once the suppler decides to take the early payment on a particular invoice, they will be paid (usually electronically) the discounted amount. Typically, this is done online using a portal approach. In fact, sometimes when you hear the term vendor portal, it will mean an invoice processing portal that includes dynamic discounting, although that is not always the case.

Inevitable the question of who provides the funding comes up. There is no simple answer. Sometimes the customer self-funds, other times there is a bank involved and more recently, some of the e-invoicing service providers, such as Basware include dynamic discounting as part of their service.

When it is not self-funded, the rate will depend on the credit worthiness of the buyer rather than the seller. This can be a real advantage in those situations where the purchaser's credit rating is significantly better than that of the seller.

Why Consider Discounting

The seller gets their cash faster thus improving their cash flow. Consequently, there is less risk of nonpayment and fewer resources spent monitoring those receivables.

For the credit, collections and receivables staff at the vendor, DSO is reduced. For some this will be an extremely important consideration. That is because for some credit folks, their bonus is calculated on how well they manage DSO. So, in these cases, there might be a real incentive to take advantage of discounting programs.

There can be some real advantages for the buyer, as well. Typically the effective rate of return is better than they would receive on other investments. This will appeal to the finance folks.

But there are benefits for the accounts payable and procure-to-pay staff as well. For starters, the requirement that invoices be approved in a timely manner takes some of the contentiousness out of their relations with other departments. The pressure to approve will come from other sources such as the suppliers themselves, management and finance.

They will have to spend less time responding to vendor inquiries, especially those where's-my-money calls. For most dynamic discounting programs include a payment status portal where vendors can see when their invoices are scheduled to be paid before deciding whether or not to take advantage of the dynamic discounting offered.

Concluding Thoughts

As you can see, there can be some real benefits to both parties when taking advantage of a dynamic discounting program. While this may not be a perfect match for every organization there are definitely pockets of applicability where it would provide a very welcome alternative. Whether it is right for your organization will take a bit of analysis and investigation to make sure you have all the pieces in place.

Chapter 23: A Word about Technology

Without a doubt, the organizations that relied heavily on technology before the COVID-19 crisis were better situated when everyone suddenly had to self-isolate. Those that were heavily reliant on paper checks often found that someone had to go into the office in order to get the payments out the door. It probably came as something of a shock to more than a few of those workers when they found their employers had labeled them as essential workers, and thus they had to go into the office.

Now, to be clear, it's not that accounts payable isn't normally essential. It most definitely is. It's just that it took a crisis of this magnitude to get many management teams to recognize that. But I digress. The point I am attempting to make is that when this is over, it is not unlikely that we'll see an explosion of technology projects at organizations of all sizes. Given that the price of much of the technology has come within the grasp of even smaller companies, no group will be exempt from this explosion.

In this section, we take a look at the following:

- Commonly-Overlooked Technology Issues that Impede AP Productivity

- Lessons Learned: Avoid These Pitfalls when Implementing an AP Technology Project

- 3 Key Technology Changes in the Accounts Payable Function

Lessons Learned: Avoid These Pitfalls when Implementing an AP Technology Project

One of the big reveals in AP Now's Technology in AP survey conducted recently was that respondents would make some big changes in the way their technology projects were implemented, if they could do it all over again. They shared their experiences so we can update you so you can avoid the headaches they experienced with their projects. Here are the top 12 problems and how you can avoid them.

1.   Terminology misunderstandings. Make sure you are on the same page with the provider when it comes to what they mean. Ask them to explain everything, even the obvious. Sometimes professionals don't ask a question because they don't want to appear foolish. That can be a costly mistake. "Topics we thought we were on the same page in our understanding proved otherwise once implemented," explained one manager.

2.   End user acceptance at other organizations. Many AP teams are good at getting their in-house partners on board but don't do much with their suppliers. If the new project will require to do additional work or something different, it is important to flush out whether or not they will cooperate. More than one project has failed when the supplier response was not taken into consideration.

3.   Where possible, take a piecemeal approach. Don't try and change everything at once, no matter how tempting that prospect may be. By implementing in small pieces, you can work out the kinks in each part before going on to the next step. Also, if one piece goes horribly wrong and you end up scrapping it, you've had a smaller disaster than if you had invested time, resources and money in a larger one.

4.   Include an adequate testing period. This can be tough because the service providers are likely to tell you that you only need a short time. Sometimes they are correct and sometimes they are not. This is one area where I'd err on the side of allowing too much time. (Same goes for training.)

5.   Have dedicated project team who can focus solely or mostly on the project at hand. If this just gets added to someone's already overflowing plate of responsibilities, the project will not get the

attention it deserves. This increases the chances that something will slip through the cracks that ultimately either dooms the project or makes it less successful than it might have been otherwise.

6. Improve communication with management about the status of the project. Unless they get regular updates, management will assume your project is proceeding on schedule without any problems. While you don't want to update them every time there is a minor issue, the sooner you alert them to a major concern that is likely to push back the start date or create another problem the better. What's more, if you try and hide it from them and they find out from someone else, your credibility on this and other projects will be severely damaged.

7. Obtain internal IT support right from the start, if you need IT involvement. Since they are usually critical to the success of your technology projects, they can't be ignored. Push hard for their support throughout the project. They have a different mindset and will often ask about issues accounting and finance don't consider. Too often, they are only brought in at the last moment and then they are less cooperative than they might have been if they had been involved from the beginning.

8. Make sure IT understands exactly what AP needs. It is critical they be involved from the start of any project that will require some IT support or help. This is true even of those technologies where AP does the heavy lifting and IT is only required to integrate the technology into the ERP and that work only takes a few hours. It is key that IT understands what AP needs and they don't try to push what they want, which may not meet AP's requirements.

9. Make sure you thoroughly understand what the technology and can do and how it will impact other departments. Ignore this issue at your own peril. "We implemented a system and within a year ripped it out," shared one manager. The encountered various unexpected headaches, departments refused to use it, slow system, and numerous duplicates and exceptions. Don't leap until you have a thorough understanding of what you are getting.

10. Make sure to find out the requirements to sync the new technology with your financial ERP, if that is required. This is one area where IT can really help. Make sure you understand before you start what

exactly will be required to get this done. Otherwise, you may have a much harder time with the new technology than you envisioned.

11. For those operating in a decentralized environment, coordinate all communications with vendors. That conversation should be addressed from a combined perspective and uniformity is required. Otherwise, suppliers will be confused and not know how to interact with different regions and will ultimately get it wrong. You could end up with more work on your hands rather than running a more effective and efficient AP operation.

12. When you have more than one ERP system, create a standard process across all business lines. Then, help the business units implement it. If each has a different process errors will slip though and those who have to deal with more than one unit will be confused. Of course, the real solution is to move to one ERP system. But that decision is not one usually made in AP.

By reviewing the issues your peers had when implementing new technology in AP, hopefully you can avoid some of the pitfalls they had to deal with. The suggestions provided will help you address the particular problem and hopefully end up with a positive outcome from your technology project.

Commonly-Overlooked Technology Issues that Impede AP Productivity

Technology can greatly enhance any accounts payable operation or it can create trouble. The trick is to make sure you get the most out of it without allowing it to wreak havoc in your accounts payable function. By making the most of your technology assets, and not letting them harm the organization, you can improve the productivity of the accounts payable function. This is critical at a time when all organizations are looking to do more with less and the accounts payable function is not exempt from that requirement. Let's take a look at three technology issues every organization should get right.

Issue #1: Full utilization of ERP capabilities. Make sure the full functionality of your ERP is being utilized. Rarely do organizations get all the value that they are paying for. This typically starts at the installation phase when all but the basic functionality is turned off. When it is finally up and running, everyone breathes a sigh of relief and forgets to go back to review what else is available.

To ensure you are fully using your accounting system's capabilities, assign at least one employee the task of fully mastering your accounting or ERP system's full set of features and functions, and have this employee regularly share this knowledge with your team of system users. To bolster his or her proficiency, the designated accounting system guru should study educational training videos, YouTube clips, books about your accounting system, blogs, professional reviews, and the vendor's end-user support pages. They might even participate in discussion forums, focused on the ERP.

 In addition, he or she should attend the vendor's annual conference and annual end-user training courses. While going through the information, don't overlook the reporting capabilities of the ERP. Are there any reports that can be automatically generated that will help? What metrics can it spit out for you, saving staff time when they no longer have to generate that information?

Issue #2: An analysis of the company website from a fraud prevention point of view. Do you have too much information on the organization's website? How is that possible, you might wonder. And what does it have to do with accounts payable? Alas, when it comes to fraud, accounts payable needs to be on top of the issue. In the past, it was a recommended best practice that companies put their ACH payment signup form for vendors on their website.

Today, thanks to some especially vicious frauds, companies are advised against taking such action unless they have a password protected site for their vendors. Then, the form can be posted, but only so approved vendors can see it. When the form is posted where everyone can view it,. For posted online it may unintentionally provide information that helps crooks perpetrate fraud on the company.

Issue #3: Regular employee education. Don't overlook employee training on a regular basis. This not only refers to the basic accounts payable procedures and technology but other areas as well. Don't forget some of the more advanced Excel options. They can be used for all sorts of analytics. This should include functions such as pivot tables, power queries, VLOOKUP, conditional formatting and more.

Some of these are quite simple to use, once you know how. They can be used to weed out duplicate payments and vendors in the master vendor file. They can also be used to identify possible fraud and for management reporting. Accounts payable was a wealth of information. It's time to mine that data and make meaningful contributions to the ongoing profitability of the organization

3 Key Technology Changes in the Accounts Payable Function

The recently conducted AP in 2020 survey revealed three key changes in the way the accounts payable function is handled at a large number of organizations. These changes represent a fundamental shift. What's more, the changes, while predominantly positive, also demonstrate that while technology continues to lead to improvements it also helps create new problems. The three findings are:

1. Use of ACH for business-to-business (B2B) payments has increased significantly; 41% of the respondents now use ACH for more than half their B2B payments.

2. Email is now the most common way invoices are delivered, with 62% saying the majority of their invoices arrive this way.

3. Duplicate submission of invoices has gotten significantly worse, with two-thirds of respondents reporting it as a serious issue.

Let's look at each in a little more detail.

Electronic Payments

There has been some real progress in the usage of ACH for B2B payments. While the percentage of organizations using ACH for B2B payments remains at the same level as in 2016 (83%), 41% report they use it for at least half of their B2B payments. This is real growth on the electronic payment front.

That being said, there is still heavy reliance on the use of paper checks. Just under half of the respondents indicated that they making at least half, if not more, of all their B2B payments using paper checks. So, there is still a lot of room for progress on the payment front. There is some cause to be optimistic about the future, in this regard. One quarter of the respondents indicated they were concerned about their organization's heavy reliance on paper checks. Recognition of the issue is the first step on the road to change.

Receipt of Invoices

Organizations continue to receive invoices various ways (most report two or three different ways), but there have been clear shifts the past few years. The big news is that the majority of invoices—no matter what the organization size—arrive electronically via email/attachments. This is a significant change from 2016 when paper/mailed invoices were most common.

There is a significant decrease in the number of organizations using fax to receive invoices. In 2016, 54% of organizations received faxed invoices at least some of the time, compared to 32% in 2019. We believe that those who still use fax receive a smaller number of invoices through this mechanism. In all likelihood, the organization is set up to receive in this manner and will continue to do so until the volume is almost non-existent or the fax machine breaks.

There were some interesting innovations related to portals. While the overall percentage of organizations using portals has declined slightly (26–27%), this has been due to a move away from home-grown models. This is a statistically insignificant number. What is quite interesting is the distinct switch to third-party portals. Use of those portals has almost doubled.

Duplicate Copies of Invoices

The most significant change in invoice headaches is the worsening issue of duplicate submission of invoices, noted by 50% of respondents in 2016, but 66% this year. That huge jump can be attributed to the rise in emailed invoices. It is just too easy for suppliers to email more than one copy of the same invoice to either different people or to accounts payable on multiple occasions.

Even if your organization is successful at identifying these duplicates and weeding them out before payment, it takes valuable resources to do so. Few companies will allocate additional staff to accounts payable to handle this. So, best to take action and minimize the problem right out of the gate. Now, without a doubt, some vendors who do this are trying to get you to pay them twice. Of course, they will never admit this and you can't accuse them of it. You just need to make sure they aren't successful.

Vendors who routinely send multiple copies of invoices should be contacted and asked to stop. Some will and some won't. What's more, once you think you have the issue under control, others will start. Or, your existing vendor will get someone new in billing and they'll decide to start sending duplicates. Basically, this is an ongoing issue that every organization will need to stay on top of. It's one of the times that technology hurts rather than helps.

A Word about Technology

As you look through the changes, both those discussed in this piece and others you've seen impacting the accounts payable function in the last few years, it is impossible not to notice that technology often plays a key role. That's why it is thought-provoking to note that several of the survey respondents' top concerns revolved around technology. Specifically, the group noted:

- A heavy reliance on manual processes 46%

- Staff won't embrace new processes or technology 36%

- Lack of use of technology 31%

- Automation's impact on AP 23%

Clearly, technology, fear of technology or lack of technology lies heavily on the minds of many. Its impact cannot be underestimated. It is the great differentiator when it comes to running an efficient and cost-effective accounts payable function and it will continue to play that role. The professionals who are concerned are right to feel the way they do.

Technology is changing the accounts payable function. It has gotten more user-friendly and less expensive and that trend continues. The silver bullet in this situation is education. Making sure that everyone learns about the new technologies is the best way to ensure the staff has the skills the need to meet the challenges of the new world. What's more, will a little education, may will lose their fear.

Concluding Thoughts

Those who shy away from learning it or embracing it are setting themselves up for disappointment in the years to come. For eventually, every company will take advantage of it. Think of it this way. Compare it to the automotive industry.

Does anyone still use a horse and buggy to get around, go to work or shopping? It is just not a realistic option. The same will be said in a few years about those who stick to their manual processes or refuse to learn about or embrace technology. While some transactional jobs will be lost, there will be a host of new ones for those who have embraced and learned the new technology.

Chapter 24: The Future: The Accounts Payable Function Post-COVID-19

If at the end of last year anyone had told you that most of the accounts payable teams would be working from home and that they had done so successfully with very little notice, you would not have believed them. If you were told that at the same time this work was being done from home, many were simultaneously home-schooling their children, you would have thought they were crackers.

But that is precisely what has happened. AP Now statistics, based on responses at a variety of AP Now sponsored events, reveal that somewhere between 85 – 95% of all accounts payable professionals are working from home. What has become patently clear, based on conversations with hundreds of professionals and managers, is that the workplace will be very different post-COVID-19. Let's take a look at five changes those working in and managing the accounts payable function can expect.

Change #1: Greater flexibility will be required. Although many accounts payable professionals are quite accommodating, as a group, a willingness to adopt change is not one of their key attributes. In fact, just the opposite is true. A good number of professionals resist new processes and try and maintain the status quo. What was learned in this crisis was that we are all able to change and when forced to do so, we can. And most were quite successful, even if the process was a little rough. Moving forward, no one knows what's around the corner. This could be a new crisis or a new technology or something no one (except maybe some science fiction writers) has yet imagined. Whatever it is, everyone in the business world, including accounts payable, needs to be ready to adapt.

Change #2: Expect to use more technology. Those who had the easiest, albeit not necessarily easy, time transitioning to a remote work environment, were those who did not have to rely on paper. Even something as simply as having invoices emailed instead of put in the postal mail helped. Early indications are that the first changes groups will make will be to adjust their processes to allow for at least some remote working and to have invoices delivered electronically, either by email or through an invoice automation solution.

 Change #3: The office itself will look very different, whether it be for the accounts payable team or other groups. Norms for social distancing will mean many have to rearrange their workspaces. This inevitably will mean that groups need more square footage, if everyone on the team is to be accommodated. Many organizations will not want to increase their financial obligations for real estate and will decide that some or, in a few cases, all of their staff will work remotely either all or part of the time.

There have been numerous reports of companies looking to reduce their physical footprint by having fewer people in the office. This will obviously translate into more remote workers. Some will only work remotely for a few days a week. Also, expect fewer in-person meetings, even when everyone is at the same physical location. As employees have become more comfortable with Zoom, Team and other online meeting protocols, these are likely to become the norm.

Lastly, certain common practices are likely to be prohibited. Forget bringing in a plate of home-baked cookies to share with your co-workers or any sort of a pot-luck or buffet lunch. Anything that involves multiple people taking food from a common utensil is not likely to be welcome ☹.

Change #4:   The process will look very different. For many this will mean a lot more technology. It will start with a greater use of existing technology. So, those with an invoice automation protocol that is only being used half-heartedly, can expect a big push to increase usage. Likewise, those who have an ACH program with a non-optimal number of vendors signed up to use it, expect a big push both from your Treasury folks and from vendors with these programs.

Probably the biggest change will come to those still receiving paper invoices. The most recent data shows that over 20% of all invoices are coming through the post of some sort (regular mail, overnight delivery etc.). Any organization not receiving 100% electronically should push their vendors to either participate in the use of an invoice automation protocol or email invoices. There is no excuse for not doing this. Those few organizations who are dealing with a regulatory requirement that paper invoices be received and/or filed should check with the regulatory body. Those requirements are fast being rewritten.

I would love to write a similar paragraph as the one above about paper checks. But that would not be accurate. While there will definitely be a move to electronic payments (ACH in the US) of some of the volume currently being paid with paper checks, it is not likely to be complete. Why do we say this? Responses from participants in some of the 10 or so events AP Now ran through late March and mid-May indicate that some will make the move, but not all. It is at the top of the To-Do list for some and not on it at all for others.

Change #5: There will be a greater recognition for the contributions made by AP staff to the overall operation of the organization. More than one AP manager has confided that their management used to be wary of letting the accounts payable staff work remotely. They were certain that the staff would goof off. But, now that they've seen that not only can the vast majority of the AP staff be trusted, they are more productive working remotely, they are changing their tune.

"Our controller has a new-found respect for the contributions the AP team made to keep the company running throughout the crisis," confided one accounts payable manager. If ever there was a tactic that smashed the stereotypical way many management teams viewed their accounts payable staff, it was the coronavirus. So, if, like me, you are looking for a silver lining to this nightmare, it may be the new way AP teams are being viewed across the country. And to my way of thinking, this is long overdue.

Concluding Thoughts

We're in uncharted territory here. Many things we take for granted are changing. In all likelihood when we come out of this, there will be more variety in the way accounts payable departments are structured and how they work. The trick for those working in the function is to stay flexible and adapt to whatever comes down the pike next. For who knows, you may just like it more than you do the status quo.

Lessons Learned

Without a doubt, this baptism by fire, of sorts, has opened a lot of people's eyes. We've all had to scramble. But, the results for many, have been surprisingly positive. They did manage to get the technology working; they did manage to get the bills paid; amazingly, most of the staff found they liked working remotely (at least part of the time); and even more surprisingly, an increasing number of management discovered and admitted their AP staff was not only competent, they could be trusted.

Let's take a look at some of the lessons learned as we move forward in what is likely to be a very different work space.

Lesson #1: We can be flexible and ready for the unexpected. No one really knows what the future holds. So, we need to expect the unexpected. The period of rapid change isn't over, in all likelihood, it is just starting. Next time we may have less notice or there may be other constraints that we have not thought of yet. But what accounts payable teams have shown through this crisis is that the team can be flexible and those that were flexible and innovative. Most were able to get their functions up and running within a week or so. Of course, there were a lot of factors that impacted the speed at which this happened. Some got up running faster than others. Those that had been already working remotely one or two days a week had a huge advantage, at least when it came to getting the technology up and running.

Moving forward we need to be adaptable and this means we need to look for new and innovative ways to run our accounts payable function. For tomorrow's office will be very different than today

Lesson #2: We need to rely on more technology with an eye towards having less paper in our offices. Without a doubt those who were using more technology had an easier time in those that were involved in a very paper-based Accounts Payable function. Moving forward we need to take a vantage of technology as much as possible as an aid to the function. So for example, we need to get away from paper. Paper invoices and paper checks created numerous problems for those who were dependent on it.

While invoice automation definitely does offer a solution, it is not the only solution. Those who are not ready to make that jump might simply consider having invoices emailed so that they're not relying on the post office to bring invoices when they may not be located in the in the office. Look for technology solutions, wherever possible. Many of them cost less than you might think. There are many of them. Some will work and some won't. Evaluate them to see what is right for your organization and fits its pocketbook.

Lesson #3: There will be new problems. One thing is certain. There will be more problems and some of these will be unexpected issues we never thought of in the past. Be ready for them. Expect them, look for them and identify them. Then create solutions. Whether they be related to the pandemic, new frauds or issues created by a changed work environment no one knows. But by being flexible and being alert you'll be able to identify the issues and create solutions that work for your organization

Lesson #4: There will be a very new and different workplace. One thing that has become increasingly apparent is that we will not be going back to the old work space we had in the past. There are issues created by new rules regarding social distancing and space needed for each employee, problems associated with mass transportation and commuting etc. All of these will lead to newer places. We may have a combo situation where people work part time at home part time in the office, some will be working completely remotely and others will only come into the office occasionally.

Already there are discussions about expanding the concept of hoteling in the workplace. This is for people who come into the office part time or occasionally. They won't have their own desk but they'll share one for the time that they're there. The whole new workplace will mean more issues and policies will have to be ironed out. All that work remains to be done.

Lesson #5: There will be a new appreciation for staffers. We also need to show some gratitude for staff both for the work that they did the last few months and for the changes that they're going to have to go through going forward. Many will have changed work routines, possibly changed hours.

Some remote working will require flexibility and adaptability on the part of the staffers. And we all know most people don't like change. For some this will be difficult we need to recognize that and make sure the staff understands that we appreciate them for doing this. In most organizations the accounts payable staff has done a phenomenal job throughout the crisis. We need to let them know that we recognize this and we appreciate them

Glossary

1099-MISC – Form used for reporting certain types of miscellaneous income paid to various parties to the IRS

1099-NEC – New IRS form used for reporting non-employee compensation to the IRS

AI – artificial intelligence

ACH – Automated Clearing House

ACH credit – An electronic payment initiated by the payor

ACH debit – An electronic payment initiated by the payee

BEC – Business Email Compromise

CFO – Chief Financial Officer

Corporate procurement card – See p-card.

Duplicate Payment – The unintentional second payment of an invoice. One type of erroneous payment and unfortunately, rarely returned by the vendor unless the customer or its audit firm discover the over payment.

Dynamic discounting – a method of payment in which payment terms are adjusted in order for the seller, at its discretion, to accelerate payment for a discount.

e-Invoice – An electronic invoice either provided through an automated approach or as simple attachment to an e-mail. Some do not consider files attached to e-mail as true electronic invoices.

Early payment discount – discount offered for early payment. Discount amount and payment terms indicated in the form of x y/net z, where x = the rate and y= the number of days when the payment is due, if discount is taken and z = due date at full amount. The most common is 2/10 net 30, allowing customers to take a 2% discount if they pay by the 10th day after the invoice date with the full amount being due 30 days after the invoice date.

Form 1099 – The Form 1099 is used to report different types of taxable income; the most common for the accounts payable groups being Form

1099MISC. This is used to report income miscellaneous income. 1099NEC – This is used to report non-employee compensation

Internal Controls - The group of policies and procedures implemented within the organization to prevent intentional or unintentional misuse of funds for unauthorized purposes.

Invoice automation – the processing of invoices in a digital environment. Sometimes the application includes AI, sometimes not.

NACHA - National Automated Clearing House Association

P-card – Credit card provided by company for use transacting company business. Sometimes referred to as corporate procurement card or purchasing card.

Purchase card – See p-card.

PO – Purchase Order

Remote working – term used to devote when the staff works outside the physical location of the employer

Telecommuting – older term that denotes remote working

TIN – Taxpayer Identification Number; for individuals it is their social security number and for entities it is their employer identification number

Travel policy – Document which outlines how an employee is to travel on company business, what is allowable and will be reimbursed and what is not. Also addresses timing requirements of when expense reports should be turned in and the process for doing so.

About Mary S. Schaeffer

Mary Schaeffer, AP Now's Founder, was recently named a top 50 Influencer in AP, by the AP Association, a global organization headquartered in the UK. She hosts the weekly AP Now podcast, which can be found on YouTube, iTunes and a variety of other podcasting networks.

Schaeffer has been creating content around the accounts payable function for 20+ years. This material takes the form of a twice-a-week free ezine, a weekly podcast, a monthly newsletter, a variety of courses for accountants, webinars, seminars and the AP Best Practice certificate program.

She has a BS in Mathematics from York College (CUNY) and a MBA in Finance from New York University. Before founding AP Now, she worked in corporate finance and treasury for Continental Grain (Cash Manager) Equitable Life, now AXA (Assistant Treasurer) and O&Y (Financial Risk Manager).

About AP Now

AP Now is a B2B niche media firm focused on creating the most-current, best-practice business intelligence around the accounts payable function. The accounts payable function represents a critical component of any accounting and finance operation as it is directly responsible for the outflow of cash.

Staying current, and therefore effective, is an ongoing challenge as:

- ✓ New frauds continually emerge,

- ✓ New technologies have the ability to make the process more efficient and

- ✓ Regulatory requirements (1099, Sales Tax, Escheat, OFAC, FCPA, 1099 reporting, TIN Solicitation etc.) change.

- ✓ And now, establishing protocols for taking the accounts payable function remote, at least part of the time.

AP Now provides its members with the latest business intelligence they need to address these challenges. This information comes from a variety of sources including in-depth practitioner surveys, specialized expert advice, IRS bulletins and more.

It is shared with members in a monthly fee-based newsletter, twice-a-month webinars, e-workshops, and a database of tips, articles and checklists.

The organization also produces a free twice-a-week ezine and a podcast. The podcast can be found on the AP Now website, iTunes, YouTube and a variety of other podcasting platforms.

For the duration of the COVID-19 crisis, AP Now partnered with the AP Association to provide weekly programs. The goal of these programs was to provide business intelligence while simultaneously helping, ever so slightly, to help morale. These were open to everyone in the accounts payable and accounting community at no cost.

Index

www.ingramcontent.com/pod-product-compliance
Lightning Source LLC
Chambersburg PA
CBHW060408220326
41598CB00023B/3058